A Church for an Open Future

A CHURCH FOR AN OPEN FUTURE

Biblical Roots and Parish Renewal

Jack W. Lundin

WITH A FOREWORD BY
Martin E. Marty

FORTRESS PRESS   •   PHILADELPHIA

Library of Congress Cataloging in Publication Data
Lundin, Jack W
        A church for an open future.
        1. Church renewal—Lutheran Church—Case studies.
2. Community of Christ the Servant—Lombard, Ill.
3. Pastoral theology—Biblical teaching. I. Title.
BV600.2.L86   262'.001   77-78634
ISBN 0-8006-1307-4

6437G77   Printed in the United States of America   1-1307

To the memory of my dad
Royal E. Lesher
who taught me to love the church

To David Granskou
friend and scholar
who taught me to love the critical quest

and

To the Community of Christ the Servant
who continue to live out that quest
with humor and compassion

Contents

Foreword

Everybody talks about biblical authority, but no one does anything about it. Well, some do. They convince themselves that they own more of it than anyone else does. They invent elaborate philosophies to prove the Bible true to their own satisfaction. It is not likely that the early Christians would have recognized much in their argument. Let the Fundamentalists unite over a dogma of scriptural inerrancy and let the Evangelicals divide over it; in either case they use the Scriptures differently than the Christian community historically did. The disputes that issue from the corners of dour and drafty seminaries, that lie inert on the pages of doleful journals, are far from the kinds of testings the biblical writings received when the church was young or on the occasions when it has been healthy.

Why the conflicts and contentions? The psychologists say that believers need total authority; if they cannot have a pope, they'll make one out of the Scriptures. Sociologists tell about how people need walls of defense against people with differing opinions. Theologians show that the disputants need a debate-stopping dyke, and nothing serves better than inerrancy. Few seem to notice that inerrancy settles nothing, that the churches which use it, though they may "clean up" in the market in an age when people seek authority and security, differ more from each other than do those who let the Bible work on them in other ways.

Other approaches are available, and Jack W. Lundin here shows how one cluster of Christians struggles with one of them. For him the issue of authority is closely connected with the question about the *use* of the Bible; its test is made in the communities that take root from the Scriptures. H. G. Wood tells of a black ministerial candidate backed to the wall by a divinity examining board whose members were split over the issue of biblical inspiration. They asked his views on it. He replied: "I think the Scriptures are sufficiently inspired for all practical purposes." Well, that's what the Bible says almost the only time it warms to the subject: "Every inspired scripture has its use for teaching the truth and refuting error, or for reformation of manners and discipline in right living" (2 Tim. 3:16, NEB).

A Church for an Open Future: Biblical Roots and Parish Renewal will remind readers of the way the early Christian community was shaped by the Scriptures even as it gave shape to them, of how the Scriptures were in the tradition and the tradition was in the Scriptures, because it shows how to read the Bible as an unfinished plot of which today's Christians are still a part. When debates over biblical authority end, no one will have proved the existence of God, solved the problem of evil, or made all sad hearts glad. But when the Bible's authority is seen in lives lived, in people inconvenienced by its message, measured by its mandates, or surprised by its grace, everything appears in a different light.

The Bible might be thought of as the "genetic programming" of the church and its parishes, the chromosomal package that determines much of their life and sets their nature free for nurture. In Lundin's view the Bible pushes the community forth on a trajectory and imparts a momentum, but it does not remove choice and change from the experience of those who take the trip. Along that trajectory, the parishioners are ready for change. Chapter 1: "In a higher world it is otherwise, but here below to live is to change, and to be perfect is to have changed often" (John Henry Newman). Nobody's perfect in this plot, but they are all growing. Disturbing as it may be to the burgeoning churches whose appeal lies in the way they have everything nailed down and walled in, the Bible is a book of change, about a God whose dealings are constant because they are grounded in His love, are changing because of the changing circumstances of his people.

Chapter 2: why not concentrate on firing the glowing core of personal and parish life rather than build a casing around it? Then, 3: know that there will be flaws and faults, and be ready for the forgiveness that helps restore community among the forgiven. Aware of faults, Pastor Lundin tells us, we can dare to be mad or improbable in the pattern of the earliest fools for Christ, followers of one who was very much at home in the world, but who walked in it with a sense of unmistakable otherness.

Worship, chapter 4, also has to derive from the biblical roots. Read the chapter and think of Romano Guardini's words: worship, the liturgy, is *"zwecklos aber doch sinnvoll."* Which, being translated for the Community of Christ the Servant and its cohorts, means that it is "pointless but significant." Apart from worship, life has too much point, too much production and grimness. Worship "signs" another order of being. 5: The concept of the covenant derives just as surely from biblical thought in the lived life of the parish; here one thinks of Luther's synonym for gospel—promise. God's promise is matched in the promises people make to each other. Education? For that there's a chapter 6, with its ingenious concept of "first confirmation," a fresh contribution to biblical nurture.

Needless to say, such a program has to end with the parish looking outward to the world. "In our era, the road to holiness necessarily passes through the world of action," says Dag Hammarskjöld. Charles Peguy was even pithier: "Everything begins in mysticism and ends in politics." Daring it is, at the present moment, to suggest again to the huddled and burrowed Christian privatists that the church has a public side, but this book dares the suggestion. Why? "Because the Bible says . . ."

We can be glad that "it seemed good to the Holy Spirit"

for people to form the Community of Christ the Servant, the intrinsic value of whose congregational life has produced great consequences for those in its range, and which, through this book by the pastor who is one of its couple of hundred ministers, will enable others to share in its biblical rootage for the sake of their own renewal.

MARTIN E. MARTY
The University of Chicago

Preface

This is not a "how to" book for beleaguered parish leaders seeking things that work! This is rather a book of descriptive theology, of questions, of options, of vulnerability to human forms, of sensitivity to how we grow in grace, of risk in the private and public arenas of the church. The Community of Christ the Servant, whose ministry I share, would be embarrassed to tears if it were to be described as a model for anyone's faith or life. Options, yes! A model, no! It is in this spirit that I would share with you, the reader, some of our experiences, questions, and learnings with respect to roots, options for change, and a working theology for today's parish.

But first a word of thanks to specific people and institutions. To David Granskou for helping to shape the crucial questions for today's church, for goodly chunks of material in this book, and for helping me rediscover that eschatological community that turns everything about the church into interesting combinations of hope, risk, and surprising grace. To Robert J. Marshall, President of the Lutheran Church in America—he was President of the LCA's Illinois Synod at the time of my beginning days at CCS—for trusting me and helping me to see and trust in a partnership of ministry which, I'm afraid, is uncommon among bishops and pastors; for being so acutely aware that there exist, in the LCA as in other denominations, Christian people who in the very integrity and intensity of their faith live out a love-hate relationship with the structured church, and for not being intimidated by such "impertinence."

My thanks to the Community of Christ the Servant, some two hundred or more men, women, and children from widely divergent backgrounds, expressing varying needs, yet willing to exercise a nonjudgmental attitude toward those who, in the faith, profess their Christianity in different ways. They ratify my faith by their very existence.

And finally, a word of thanks to so many "friends of the Community": to Martin Marty for his valuable counsel and support, for the many days spent with us as vital resource, for being along with Elsa and the Marty boys a part of our wider "family"; to Elmer Witt, Granger Westberg, Philip Anderson, Joseph Sittler, and Bob Shaner for influencing our corporate lives; to Robert Benne, Philip Hefner, David Lindberg, Walter Michel, Franklin Sherman, and Robert Tobias, all of the Lutheran School of Theology at Chicago, who made major contributions as teachers and occasional theologians at CCS. My thanks to those who in one way or another have been identified as part of the occasional pastoral staff of CCS over the past eight years: to Gary Rowe, United Church of Christ minister, who for four years was our minister in arts and media and who provided us with appreciation for the poetry within our faith, and to Tom Peyton, Maryknoll priest and our occasional "minister to political change." Thanks also to Carole Ahlberg for patience in reading my scribbled manuscript and typing it all up, to Robert Allenson and Ruth Beales for proofreading, and finally to the many many people who helped us laugh at ourselves and our presumptions as we experimented with the very serious business of discovery through relationship.

A Church for an Open Future

Introduction

As far back as 1970 there were sometimes playful and sometimes serious suggestions that the experiment known as the Community of Christ the Servant be written up, described, or at least made reportable to the Lutheran Church in America. From its inception it was to be "an experimental expression" of the parent LCA in west suburban Chicago. It was to be an alternative to the normative parish, a place for those caught in a love-hate relationship with the church.

It was to be vividly ecumenical. The name of the congregation left no doubt. The denominational name was appended to it in parentheses as if to say: we are a servant community in Christ, and our heritage and theological context is Lutheran.

It was to be a place where important questions, even doubts, were expected to be raised. In other words, it was to be a church in the radical and probing sense, where seeking roots is considered an important quest, where theology becomes better known and more exciting than the budget or the number of communicants on the rolls.

It was to be issue-oriented. That would mean paying more attention to the building of human structures around human hurts, needs, and desires than to filling out the intramural requirements and categories of the constitution's standing committees. It would mean becoming involved in neighborhood and world, and, as we would soon discover,

1

becoming "Christ incognito" within political organizations and existing power structures all around us.

It was to touch base with the very deepest of Christian roots—liturgical, educational, theological, methodological—in order to allow such roots to speak to, for, and against present thinking and parish practice.

It was to take seriously the redefining of roles, lay and pastoral. This would mean equipping the laity to genuinely "own" ministry of some consequence. It would also mean encouraging the professional minister in his or her role as theologian-in-residence as well as enabler of authentic ministry on the part of laity.

It was to be a sensitive community of believers: sensitive to each other's needs, and in that regard careful about judging the level of faith and practice in others, sensitive to the American church's predisposition to say "bigger is better" and so to lose one another in typical big-parish anonymity. But sensitive too in the performance of a noncoercive evangelism and a form of stewardship which might allow each member a voice and a vote on how issues, cares, and benevolences translate from communications *about* such concerns to actual commitments *toward* them.

It was to be a community of people who might allow for honest doubt to act as a mysterious and grace-ful prelude to the possibility of real faith. It was, therefore, to be a catholic kind of church, diverse in scope, intention, promise, and risk.

It was to be a group of people willing to risk the freedom to laugh and cry with each other as well as to engage in a human openness which would not hide nor apologize for our being vulnerable.

It was somehow—and possibly above all else—to become a community of hope, an eschatological people standing on their tiptoes in anticipation of the marvelous actions of God's graces yet to come! It would be held together by the Eucharist: a forgiven and forgiving, nonjudging, and highly supportive therapeutic people.

All that? It all seemed so basic, so necessary, so excitingly rooted in the tradition of the church. Some of it would surely rub cross-grain with *recent* tradition to be sure. We found from the very first that words like "experimental," "noncoercive," "ownership of ministry," and "issue-oriented stewardship" caused those involved to gradually shape and then reshape, probe, and question their own commitments and ministries until there was usually a well-considered and highly personalized as well as corporate *apologia* for proclaiming themselves as Christians.

From the first, no one connected with the Community of Christ the Servant seemed to have the time or motivation for reporting on the experiment. The fun and excitement was in the doing, not in the reporting. Besides, there were nearly always available to us short and enjoyable forums for reporting of a kind—clergy workshops, visits from lay leadership groups, seminars, informal discussions ranging from an hour after the Sunday liturgy to a full week of in-residence study by clergy selected every year from around the country. All such events meant, for us at least, an opportunity for reporting—as well as for sharing the life of the Community and exploring together those theological roots which concerned everyone interested in parish renewal.

It should be quickly added that CCS confronted right from the first, and with accustomed reluctance, its failures as well as its successes. Indeed, the terms "failure" and "success" are far too imprecise to describe a living organism, especially a church which is attempting to do the will of the Father. Both pastor and people often learned more and grew more definedly in grace from the ideas and programs which did not work! Particularly at such times, the characterization of a local parish as "an experimenting expression" can indeed become freeing for the people involved. For some congregations near the geographic gathering-place of CCS the notion of experimentation meant that some of their members would take a few years out to try the different parish programming of CCS, feed back some results, and

then rejoin the normative parish after bidding fellow ex-
perimenters a fond good-bye. For others more suspicious it
meant a distinct separation by a small group of dissenters,
more pointedly, people who were nearly always fighting institutions. The fact that CCS had its genesis in the summer
of '68 in—of all discordant communities—the Chicago
metropolitan area gave fuel to such an erroneous notion.

The idea of experimentation was and is, for CCS, the
very crux of the church's self-understanding as an historic
institution. One of our Advent Liturgies, paraphrasing
Jürgen Moltmann's *Theology of Hope*, puts it this way:

> From first to last and not merely in the epilogue, Christianity
> is eschatology, is hope, forward looking and forward moving,
> and therefore its members are always revolutionizing and
> transforming the present. Hope is not one element of Chris-
> tianity but is the medium of Christian faith as such and the
> key in which everything in it is set. Be now that human
> medium and that key toward your fellow human, knowing
> that you are free in Christ to do so.[1]

To experiment is to live, to be open to the future. Very
early in our development, in a Sunday morning post-liturgy
conversation, Martin Marty helped us adopt an attitude
toward living out of an eschatological dimension. He
quoted from a recent Pogo cartoon which says, "We've got
faults we haven't even used yet." That was it! Since that
day the pithy truth of Pogo has adorned our walls wherever
we have rented, borrowed, or cajoled space for the worshiping community.

Our search for roots not only helps us describe why we
do the things we do as Christians, but often causes us either
to change doing what we've been doing, or more radically,
to find deeper and more critical roots which alter both mind-
set and life-style.

David Granskou, New Testament scholar and teacher,
entered into the life of CCS from the very first days, helping

---

1. Jack Lundin, *Liturgies from the Community of Christ the Servant*
(Downers Grove: CCS Publishing House, 1975) , p. 12.

us set forth the critical christological questions, causing us to open the Scripture and judge for ourselves what it was saying. In a real sense Granskou gave the grass roots Christian a theological birthright, a confidence in the handling of ancient truths, a freedom to raise questions and make interpretations consistent with good scholarship and devoid of pietistic glossing. We began a continuing struggle to take seriously the critical questions of biblical scholarship and theological inquiry. "What does this mean for us?" we asked. "Can we *own* it?" "Is it genuinely noncoercive?" These questions are frequently asked around CCS as we seek to probe, for example, the early church's appreciation of the Eucharist, as well as our entire theological heritage and historic roots.

The excitement and expectation inherent in the good news of Jesus Christ can be released—here and now—without gimmickry, hard-sell Fundamentalism, or the kind of preaching which plays on the emotions. For CCS it happens by touching base with roots, by asking questions, by letting history and tradition become ours rather than just something remote, reserved only for understanding scholars! It also happens by letting doubts be articulated, and taken seriously, even as doubts are part of the very structure and content of faith. The "Christ is the answer" crowd may be winning many new converts, but there are some of us, probably a minority, who are still impertinent enough to say: "But what is the question?"—and in that inquiry to touch the very hem of him whose appreciation of the question and its power guided his life and ministry.

So, on with the inquiry: to discover our roots and be open to our future, to locate answers and securities wherever they may be found, knowing that new questions will repeatedly need to be asked when formerly dependable and comfortable structures no longer seem to function for us, possibly because they no longer function for God. Indeed, the *process* may be more significant than any of the (still workable?) parish programming illustrated in the chapters of this book.

Prologue:
An Experimental Expression—
The Community of
Christ the Servant

This Prologue is excerpted from a year-by-year journal of events in the life of that "experimental expression of the Lutheran Church in America" known as the Community of Christ the Servant, a community of annually covenanting people from over forty cities and towns in five counties in and around Chicago. This historical sketch will provide background for the following seven chapters with their exploration of a theological base and rationale for an experimental style of life in today's parish.

(Jan., 1968) Jack W. Lundin meets with denominational officials to begin shaping a possible experiment based upon the LCA's purchase of expensive property directly across from one of the country's newest and largest indoor-shopping centers, Yorktown in suburban Lombard, directly west of the city of Chicago.

(Mar.) Feasibility study on the property determines that it is "too valuable to build a church on" (reactions range from amused to confused). LCA decides to go with "whatever may develop," considering data as well as church's hope to see some creative expression of its mission at that place. Intention is to allow for development of a local mission oriented toward openness and experimentation.

(Apr.) Lundin meets with west suburban LCA pastors to describe experimental intentions, seek support, and allow for questions and objections. Good open dialogue ensues.

(June) Lundins move to Lombard on the 15th to begin

work. The name Community of Christ the Servant is adapted from Philippians 2:7, "Christ . . . emptied himself, taking the form of a servant." *Community* is substituted for *church,* a term usually associated with bricks and mortar, a building rather than a people.

(June) Lundin completes a three-year graduate program at school in Geneva, Switzerland, and in the Chicago area, feeling that many Christians are sublimating through acceptable structures a love-hate relationship not only with church as institution but also with God, and that the dialectic is an honest one that needs to be raised up to the level of practicable parish life.

(June) Experimental themes are set and given good local and regional press:

1. Imaginative use of property rather than building an expensive, little-used edifice exclusively for the congregation.
2. Worship in accordance with tradition, maintaining catholic form and content, yet free to utilize variety in setting forth ancient and contemporary themes. Worship may be a didactic tool but must always invite into the mystery which it celebrates in Christ.
3. Education which will avoid ready-made answers. Because questioning is an inherent gift from Jesus' own rabbinic style, we also question in order to seek deeper truth. This includes questioning "traditional" forms like Sunday school.
4. The theme of servanthood will not only include the role of ombudsman alongside the traditional roles of benevolent welfare programming, but also the more risky role of social activist.

(July) First worship is held at Bethany Seminary Chapel, Oak Brook, Illinois, on the 28th. The pre-worship introductions and reiteration of experimental hopes and dreams gradually develop into a pre-liturgy time for mutual discussion of politics, community life, and decisional issues.

(Aug.) Begin to invite area personalities and theologians in for "inquiry" sessions in theology and structure. "How parents may best become their children's teachers," discussed by Freda Kehm of CBS radio, is found to be a very delicate issue since most parents apparently feel inadequate, especially as *Christian* educators of their own children.

(Fall) A "supportive" program for parents is begun as a substitute for Sunday school. We would not usurp parental prerogatives to educate their children. We begin a "Wednesday Children's Program" each week for an hour after school, visceral rather than cerebral in nature, with a group of nurturing adults who had to unlearn the role of "teacher" and becomes *themselves* the live resources. We felt that little children may not care if "Jesus loves them" or if a book tells them so, but that they will be moved if a human being, acting in Jesus' name, actually picks them up and loves them!

(Sept.) A series of six christological inquiries led by David Granskou sets an important theological base for an embryonic searching community.

(Sept.) The LCA Manifesto, a contemporary commentary on continuing reformation, is studied with great benefit. We wondered what might occur if congregations—if we—took the Manifesto seriously.

(Oct.) With the trauma in and around the Democratic National Convention—riots, macings, clergy-police confrontations—and with the nation suffering from assassinations and from humiliation in a war that was becoming a threat to our basic unity as a people, we participate, through the pre-liturgy issue process, in marches and protests, and in services of humiliation, penitence, prayer, and reconciliation, and generally anguish openly in our prayers, dialogue, and sermons over our corporate identity as God's children in this place and in this time.

(Oct.) On the 13th we open a "Covenant" together. Worshipers tell of their inadequate pictures of God and Scripture, instilled in them during childhood and youth and, tragically, never again confronted or challenged to renewal and maturity. We determine together to *create* an occasion when we will be forced to wrestle with the angel (as Jacob did in Genesis 32). In order to reassess, grow, and struggle for the meaning of our faith, membership will be predicated on a process of annual "release." A frightened pastor could envision a time when all the members, instead of bothering to struggle for fresh meaning, would simply quit. That has not yet happened.

(Oct.) On the 27th a dialogue sermon with Fr. Larry Connors, S.J., teacher of ethics at St. Louis University, provides a "necessary" contact for Protestants on "Reformation Sunday," especially for those whose view and understanding of reformation is couched only in sixteenth century images.

(Nov.) An old barn and farmhouse situated on the "too expensive . . ." property is converted into a church for temporary use. Little did we realize how much attention that would evoke—a church worshiping in a barn! Articles appear in *The Lutheran* and later in *Time* magazine, to name a few, describing, quite inadvertently, the experimental programming going on in such a crude setting (especially attractive at Christmas). Worship in the barn begins on a cold Christmas Eve. It is drafty and of necessity candlelit, with straw and mangers quite authentic.

(Jan., 1969) More adult theology offered in lieu of "traditional Sunday school." Some nearly panic when that 200-year-old structure is removed and nothing is left in its place but adult (parental) learning.

(Jan.) Musicians, particularly professional jazz players, are invited to the Sunday liturgies in the Barn. They are allowed to make their offerings through their creative music with no conditions set, no instructions given, no boundaries imposed. They appreciate the church viewing their art as a legitimate expression of their being, as if it actually counted and had some depth of meaning.

(Feb.) The gutbucket chorus is created in and through the Wednesday Children's Program. Some, too young to read the words of the hymns, can nevertheless pull on the strings attached to a broomstick and grounded by a colorfully painted topsy-turvy washtub. The kids "own" a bit more of worship.

(Mar.) Burrell Gluskin joins the CCS staff, largely unpaid. Jewish, with Christian sensitivities, Burrell creates the "throwaway choir" for those who may sing on special occasions but do not wish to commit every Thursday to rehearsals, a "participatory anthem" which allows everyone to play rhythm instruments while singing, and a series of children's hymns touching themes nearly forgotten in today's churches like "imagination," "nonsense," "my body," "animals," "friends," and many more which we are soon compelled to publish.

(May) We plunge into cantatas with throwaway choirs and professional jazz players; and painting the inside walls of the barn according to our "faith-views" at the invitation of artist Carl Johnson; and searching out the history and tradition behind certain liturgical days.

(May) We find ourselves developing a Youth Help Center (and training a dozen people as crisis phone-answerers), a ministry which a year later we turned over to a neighboring group which made it their full-time business to care for teens on drugs or having problems.

(Spring) "Imagi Theater," a group of creative teens wishing to do more than coffeehouse events, hold "Edward Albee" evenings and even do plays of their own. Some Saturday evenings see nearly 200 filling the Barn for purposes of exchanging budding poetic and artistic urges. Paul Firnhaber, formerly a youth director of the Lutheran Church, Missouri Synod, is engaged to be their supportive friend. The program, in a variety of stages, lasts about two years.

(Spring) We hold our first pre-Holy Week enactment of the Jewish "seder," the holy meal of the Passover. Using Lundin's brief and instructive commentary for Christians wishing to sense the historic occasion of the Last Supper, we begin a tradition which will continue each year on Palm Sunday evening, ending with the "Hava Nagila."

(Summer) The first of a continuing series of out-of-town and out-of-country guest pastors and theologians arrive to stay with covenant members for a few days at a time as part of a mutual learning process. John Lyons from St. Olaf College shows us how filmmaking can become a familiar artistic/faith expression for small children at CCS.

(Fall) We make fast friends with a Roman Catholic experimental "non-parish" known as REC (Religious Education Center) and its pastor, Fr. Tom Peyton, who commits himself to political change in Du Page County where CCS is headquartered. Tom becomes, unofficially, our "Minister to Political Change."

(Sept.) On the 7th, during a Sunday dialogue on the nature of the church, we suddenly *all* seem convinced that the church is fed as well as defined by both word *and* sacrament. At the end of the dialogue and just before the "Kiss of Peace" a worshiper yells out, "Somebody quick get the bread and wine." We have never been without the Eucharist since that day!

(Dec.) We "disband" in order to "wrestle with the angel" and to have the freedom to make new covenants for the year ahead, a year of inquiry into our roots, surprises in our Sunday liturgies, solidifying friendships, adding staff, and reaching out in many new directions.

(Jan., 1970) Joining Martin Marty and David Granskou as good friends and generous supporters of our common guests and experiences are Jim Murray, a gutbucket-playing Presbyterian seminarian from McCormick Seminary in Chicago, and Pete Steinke, an LC, MS pastor working on his doctorate and willing to commit fifteen months of "field experience" time as youth minister. We finally get up enough nerve to add as a paid "Minister in Arts and Media" Gary Rowe, a 1970 graduate of Bethany Seminary. We manage to "put together a salary package" with CCS funding and support from his denomination, the United Church of

Christ, and from the Church of the Brethren for experimental work in video-oriented curriculum for children. Gary is ordained in the Barn on 9 June 1970. What a celebration!

(Spring) The Chicago affiliate of NBC-TV does an on-location series of six half-hour tapes about CCS. It is our first taste of bright lights, camera lens down our throats—all the while attempting to maintain what the director called a combination of "attentive coolness and spontaneous intimacy." It doesn't work. We come off as stiff and scared—because we are! The TV critics, expecting "religious news" to turn more spritely, are unimpressed. We are exhausted. All in all, the experience helps us keep defining, keep pressing the questions.

(May) CCS becomes an official congregation of the Illinois Synod of the LCA. Some thought the affiliation meant that after experimenting for a brief time we were now to "go normative." Not so. We feel that "Christian normative" *keeps* experimenting.

(Spring) Our little booklets of original liturgies and new hymns in the jazz or swing motif are being stolen by the hundreds—a compliment that was simply too expensive for us to afford. Interested people form a not-for-profit CCS publishing house, first publishing Lundin's *Little Liturgies for the Christian Family*, a booklet used to facilitate Christian celebration of family-oriented events such as birthdays, baptismal birthdays, making-up, wedding anniversaries, homecoming, and welcoming overnight guests. It even includes a home communion called "Family Eucharist," celebrated on certain Thursday evenings at CCS as a "Kitchen Communion." The Kitchen Communion Eucharist helps CCS people focus on neighborhoods, local needs, and bringing people together who live close by.

(Fall) We help establish the Lombard chapter of HOPE (Homes of Private Enterprise), an open-housing group who also helped the poor purchase their own homes in Du Page county, fourth wealthiest in the nation. We fill the old four-truck milk garage on the Barn property with used furniture, appliances, clothing, and food staples for the needy—four times over in a year's time.

(Oct.) We begin what proves to be a four-year cooperative venture, the Suburban Training Center, with Pastor Gary Rowe as director. CCS is the "center," the "training" being direct involvement in nonparish forms of ministry for students of the sponsoring institutions: the Evangelical Seminary (United Methodist), Bethany (Church of the Brethren), Northern Baptist, and, informally, for students from De Andreas (Roman Catholic), McCormick (Presbyterian), and Lutheran School of Theology. Areas of involvement include: defining Suburban Matrix, studying law enforcement, working with legal problems and civil liberties (from 1969 on, CCS housed the Du Page office of the American Civil Liberties Union, first at the Barn and then wherever CCS moved), coffeehouse ministries, street ministries to youth, political action groups, consumer protection groups, and fair housing concerns.

(March, 1971) With the Vietnam War festering, we help sponsor a public appearance by Dr. Eqbal Ahmad, a Third World spokesman and scholar from the Stevenson Institute. Some Du Page people feel CCS should be "watched." We try not to become paranoid about being openly against the war.

(Mar.) The Lutheran Human Relations Association shows at the Barn the Canadian TV film dealing with the killing of Fred Hampton, Black Panther.

(Apr.) Eighteen musicians in big-band style conduct Good Friday service at the Barn. They play musical expressions reflecting seven human reactions/projections to death. Who ever heard of packing them in on Good Friday? We turn away over 100 people.

(Apr.) Suburban Training Center is awarded $65,000 by the Irwin-Sweeney-Miller Foundation to carry on a two-year "Project Understanding" among and in cooperation with dozens of suburban churches, focusing on the theme of racism in suburbia. Vestiges of the organization live on in new forms in the Downers Grove area today.

(May) On the 16th the Roman Catholic experimental community (REC) joins CCS at the Barn and stays with us until we leave to go on our nearly three-year pilgrimage. They hold their mass an hour after ours. Sometimes we share word and sacrament together.

(May) Seventeen pastors come to live with us for a week as we hold our first Pastors' Live-in Workshop in Parish Renewal. Feeling that we might, by now, provide experiential feedback to the LCA on being an "experimental expression," and also wishing to receive critical review, we work with the denominational leadership responsible for continuing clergy education to provide resource people and to invite selected clergy to join in a common search for renewal. CCS members and friends find it is enlightening and exhausting, but fun. The week-long workshops, highly visceral, are continued each year, to the special delight of members who house the visiting clergy.

(Aug.) The 22nd is our last day at the Barn, which will give way to a new executive office complex. The Barn, the milk truck garage, and the farmhouse which had housed offices, classrooms, counseling rooms, and even a "draw-all-over-the-walls" expression room—all have to go. For this last Sunday Burrell writes a dirge called "The Barn is Dead"; we all sing with tear-filled eyes. Then, dancing the "Lord of the Dance," we send ballooned messages sky-high as love notes from a "neat place to be."

(Aug.) On the 29th we move in with fellow Lutherans at St. Luke's Church in Glen Ellyn, only a few miles west of the Barn. They are pastorless, in some need of the monthly rental we will pay, and willing to risk a live-in with an alternative life-style congregation. Though it is never a full marriage, the year-long venture in trust provides a mutual learning experience and teaches us all a sense of tolerance and patience. CCS is to be what our new liturgy for that August Sunday taught us: "A Pilgrim People."

(Aug.) The CCS Repertory Theater Company emerges with Pastor Rowe leading people in fresh expressions of life-values through drama. His work with whole families in improvisational theater and with children in video-cassette education for the Christian classroom involves good numbers of willing people at CCS.

(Summer) Amid fanfare, cameras, press coverage, and hoopla, the Concerned Citizens of Du Page come into being when the Chicago Indian Village moves to our county to stake claims on government ground at Argonne National Research Laboratories. We attempted to act as ombudsman for the Indian group but at the time had little or no idea how to establish a viable community organization. The plight of the American Indian is light-years behind that of any other visible American minority. We met countless hundreds of sympathetic county people—all convening around the Indian issue and all "finding each other" as we discovered our own helplessness in the face of a national disaster among native Americans.

(Oct.) Our Volunteers in Publishing is born. Publishing liturgy books and new hymnals requires volunteer help to publicize, receive orders, do mailings, and things only truly dedicated people may be made to do in the name of an idea or hope which they wish to share. VIPs continue on bravely.

(Fall) Our political sensitivities are sharpened in pre-liturgy format when Paul Simon and Dan Walker, articulate rival Democratic candidates for Governor of Illinois, agree to speak to us on separate Sunday mornings. They do. We benefit.

(Fall) The Children's Program holds the first annual "glue-in," with imagination running high as small children glue chips and odd-sized pieces of lumber and shavings together in interpretive sculpting. We also have "share a pet" day; live pets are brought in somehow—in a cage, on a leash, in a bowl. All are blessed, loved, and identified as significant "people" in young lives. It seems important that they *too* get to go to church once in a while.

(Nov.) Right up until Christmas, many of us are helping Arthur Allen and Kenan Heise promote their *Death of Christmas*, a sensitive little book of Christmas Eve interviews with the disfranchised and discouraged. It helps us focus the loneliest season in the calendar on themes of mercy, justice, and sharable love.

(Nov.) Lundin's *Celebrations* is published in New York. We have a party, naturally. At CCS celebrations happen at the drop of a hat.

(Jan., 1972) Our Ministry to Freedom of the Press publishes the first issue of "Press Relief." Chicago *Sun-Times* columnist Roy Larson makes a revealing presentation concerning government controls on American press freedoms.

(Jan.) Making chalices for our homes proves to be a warm, family-oriented project.

(Jan.) On the 30th CCS Publishing House introduces *Liturgies for Life* by Lundin and Gluskin.

(Feb.) The ever-expanding adult theology series now encompasses the use of resource people in about thirty deep and serious short-term courses each year. Living through Chicago winters seems reason enough for introducing a new two-session course on "Wine tasting for Christians and other bons vivants." It always has full registration.

(Feb.) On the 14th we hear Levi Ben Israel, leader of the Chicago-based Black Israelites. In two weeks we helped raise over $1,000 after discovering their need and how effective they are in dealing with riots, crime, and drug traffic in Chicago's near West side. Denominational people alert us to the possibility of such support with the comment, "Christians don't usually put black Jews into their budgets."

(Mar.) We inaugurate a short-lived program called "the other child" into our regular Wednesday children's supportive education series. The "other child" refers to the mentally or emotionally handicapped youngster who, by being isolated from normally developing children and having no one to imitate except himself, often recedes even further into his unique situation. Parents of such children often wish normal situations were available to their children. We attempted to provide such an atmosphere and discovered that we were not able to put our efforts into such a thoroughly demanding enterprise.

(Apr.) Our second annual Pastoral Workshop in Parish Renewal proves to be a glorious time.

(June) A twelve-day serendipity trip takes our teens, en route to the East Coast via Canada, right through the middle of Hurricane Agnes! Sponsors and pastor barely survive.

(July) We move again. This time from St. Luke's Lutheran to St. Barnabas Episcopal, also in Glen Ellyn. By now we are used to watching for how we "drop our dirty socks" in various places. A book could be written on the problems and possibilities of two congregations sharing the same building.

(Aug.) We test the water of an apartment house ministry. Apartment house managers tell us what is happening, and we are convinced that the churches have unique ministries to apartment dwellers. We begin to work with seven sister congregations in the initial development of a brochure which tells of the special gifts and emphases of our respective parishes. But then we never get much beyond that. In this as in various of our other ministries, "we've got faults we haven't used yet."

(Oct.) On the 8th the cast from *Godspell*, playing at the Blackstone Theater in Chicago, blends their songs and choreography into the fabric of the morning Eucharist. Cast and congregation minister to each other. We are all surprised to learn how well their musical translates the basic themes of liturgy.

(Oct.) We plan with Granger Westberg to implement his Wholistic Health clinic concept for churches, utilizing a minimum of square footage, to operate a health care clinic with resident physician and counselor as soon as possible.

(Oct.) Many CCS people become actively involved in the presidential elections, with most sentiment going not to the incumbent but to the challenger, at least as a way to keep raising questions.

(Oct.) The fact that we welcome well-known war protesters to special evenings at CCS leads to protests, angry calls from as far away as Iowa, and even death threats for the better part of a week. Our way of keeping urgent questions alive also displeases some of the leaders of St. Barnabas, where we are, after all, merely renters.

(Dec.) Our annual procedure of disbanding and wrestling with the angel before we commit ourselves to a new set of covenants with God and with each other has never seemed routine, and is far from routine this year. We begin to develop liturgical assists for dealing with the biblical models and theological implications of our strenuous involvements.

(Feb., 1973) We move from St. Barnabas Episcopal, which now has its new rector and is rapidly expanding its program. It is only a matter of months before we will be able to move back to the Barn—this time a new "barn" in the shape of a five-story office complex called Yorktown Executive Plaza, so we make arrangements for interim housing with Mt. Calvary Methodist Church in Lombard, a small mission which is nearly ready to close its doors and merge with its larger sister-congregation in downtown Lombard. On the 8th, feeling very much the pilgrim people, we move sign, piano, office equipment, chalices, bean bags, and people. How many more nail holes can our outdoor sign take?

(Apr.) We ratify an agreement with the church-at-large for a long-term occupancy in Yorktown Executive Plaza.

(Aug.) Mt. Calvary sells its building to Congregation Etz Chaim. We meet the new rabbi and plan again to move.

(Aug.) Part of a frustrating month is spent headquartered at the Holiday Inn, Oakbrook Terrace. The office of the church now overlooks the swimming pool. Nice, but expensive.

(Sept.) On the 9th we move into Yorktown, occupying 4,000 square feet of main-floor space on the ground of what was once the Barn property.

(Sept.) On the 30th all covenant members are invited to paint their "faith expressions" on the interior walls of the worship area. We begin to locate offices, a CCS Publishing House area, a "Commons" for teaching and meeting purposes, and a media center. It begins to look like home.

(Oct.) We decide to hold the third annual Pastors' Workshop a year later—too much activity just moving from place to place in 1973.

(Dec.) We begin a whole new ministry to professional jazz musicians and a regular Sunday Jazz Vespers at which musicians may express their faith through their talent without it being a typical "gig." The three o'clock "congregation" becomes a strange and beautiful new world of creative and artistic people.

(Feb., 1974) New liturgical expressions begin accumulating with the help of an increasing number of CCS people interested in history, theology, and liturgical expression. *Liturgies from the Community of Christ the Servant* documents the fruits of a testing process for Christian expression.

(Feb.) The teens take a four-day serendipity trip to Washington, D.C., this time by Amtrak and air. We probe into political workings at the national level, raising questions and finding more questions to raise in return.

(Apr.) A pastoral workshop in the theology of evangelism follows the abortive attempt of hard-sell evangelism via "Key '73." Why is it so difficult to talk about evangelism and theology at the same time and with the same people?

(Aug.) Accountant David Veatch, a CCS member and well-informed theologian fresh from a denominationally funded year of training at the Industrial Areas Foundation in Chicago, has denominational seed money to do issue-oriented community organizing in suburbia, where "enlightened self-interest" may not automatically issue in a drive for such basics as food, clothing, and housing. Initially community organization begins to develop around the "hot" issue of flooding, and the Flood Land Action Campaign (FLAC) gradually takes shape, home-owners' associations and teachers' unions joining with local parishes encompassing three or four major denominations. Targeted for immediate "action" are the county zoning boards who exploit for the sake of "progress" and expansion.

(Sept.) The liturgical deacons and liturgical writing group take serious notice of the call toward inclusive language. Male-oriented liturgies are revised and the "ownership" of worship in format, leadership, language, and theme begins to concern more people.

(Sept.) A new teaching liturgy for the day of St. John Chrysostom enables us to "plunge" into the world of Eastern Orthodoxy, with Robert Tobias as a guide. Our demonstration and teaching liturgy was followed by a Greek feast complete with roast pig and lamb, salads filled with feta cheese, flaming cheese, sticky desserts, and resin-filled Greek wine.

(Oct.) We develop a new sensitivity to the growing number of singles at CCS and in our immediate area; the unmarried, divorced, and widowed as well as those who came to CCS singly, without the entire family. A church welfare agency and a fraternal insurance company help underwrite an experiment in relating singleness and church. In a weekend workshop attended by nearly a hundred singles and church resource people we tried to help singles feel comfortable in and with the church, and the church understand and deliberately include in ministry those who are single. Important feedback guided us to thoughts about another try next year.

(Fall) Lundin becomes regular host for "Of Cabbages and Kings" on Chicago's ABC-TV station, an issue-oriented public affairs show.

(Jan., 1975) FLAC becomes FLAC I (Flood Land Action Campaign) and FLAC II (Fair Land Assessment Campaign) when another suburban issue comes to the fore. All the makings of a genuine community organization begin to surface, and mostly because we are able for the first time in the memory of any of us to see concerned church people "in action," going before land developers, county boards, and tax assessors to demand records, uncover corruption, and actually have a visible hand in reshaping our neighborhoods and our county affairs. We keep asking: Who are we, as Christians, in all of this?

(May) FLAC I and FLAC II become the Du Page Citizens Organization, made up of many dozens of groups of teachers' organizations, churches, home-owners' associations, and other groups. The DCO even includes the retired, the so-called gray panthers, who, like the rest of us, were angry about having no say, power, or participation in a local government so used to having its own way as a one-party system.

(May) Along with the ACLU and the DCO, the Du Page County Chapter of the National Organization of Women now meets at CCS. The Du Page Mental Health Association requests free office space at CCS. We vote yes, aware of the church's responsibility to act in tandem and thus in ministry with concerned groups of "issue" people such as these.

(Fall) As always, we receive more from the visiting clergy than we give at our Third Annual Pastors' Workshop.

(Fall) On the Sunday of Michelangelo's birthday his paintings abound and we remember his heritage and message through liturgy. Family Film Nights with their relaxing potluck and good movies prove therapeutic for those with small children who lament all the Rs and Xs at the local cinema. The CCS Campers plan three Sundays out in the woods, with Eucharist and fun, sleeping late and good conversation; noncampers keep the doors open at CCS those Sundays and we pray for each other.

(Fall) Julian Adderley's friends come the Sunday following the "Cannonball's" death; their expressions of grief and their tribute to him as a man and an artist helped the CCS morning covenant crowd understand and empathize with the afternoon non-CCS musicians crowd.

(Jan., 1976) Our denomination's director of Planning and Research comes to the Chicago area to get acquainted and to examine our style of ministry. Seven other congregations are also to be used in a research-and-tell model, then perhaps more and more congregations as the need for such sharing is evidenced around the church. Al Haversat helps us in the necessary business of continual reassessment. Any congregation six (officially) or eight (actually) years old—experimental or not—needs both time and occasion to seek out its ruts (as well as its roots) lest it stay comfortable within them.

(Feb.) One of the most joyous and rewarding moments in our history occurred the day we met at O'Hare Airport the plane from Santiago, Chile. On it was Yamil Ahuile, straight from the Chilean concentration camp, together with his wife Sonia, their daughter Tati, and their younger son Yamilito. Once a university teacher, in a position of respect in that land's utility company, Yamil was, without warrant and without trial, accused of being on the "wrong" side of the junta which overthrew the Allende regime. He spent over a year in five different camps while the family was reduced to poverty, selling the children's toys and clothes to make ends meet. Our "Statement of Concern" of a year earlier had helped release a trickle of selected prisoners (named by deposed Bishop Helmut Frenz) and the Ahuiles were just the second family destined for the U.S. to be allowed their freedom. When Yamil and Sonia were reunited by the Chilean government they were seated next to each other and their children for the first time in over a year. After the overnight flight they immediately became "refugees" and wards of CCS. We were tearful and stunned by the reality of such human pathos in our very midst. It softened whatever residue of hardened political apathy we might have had. They became "one of us," worshiping and sharing love in great depth. CCS will never be the same— thank God!

(Winter) Because we had been routinely requesting prayers of intercession for "all sorts and conditions," and especially those conditions which afflict real, nameable people, we found ourselves moved to deal with the pain of separated and divorced couples. Before the prayers, the pastor, with the permission of the couple, asks for all present to acknowledge the pain of those who are suffering it—in whatever form it may then be—and to openly *be* a therapeutic, caring community for and with those people, offering them support and a sense of neutrality while they recover from the shock and hurt of a world caving in on them. The Divorce Support Group was formed, meeting regularly with a trained convener, Brenda Wanner, a practicing psychologist and CCS member, who was herself divorced.

(Spring) The resurgent interest in Bible study and interpretation is enough to warm the cockles of a pastor's heart. Nearly fifty adults participating in two separate "tracks" of study on the parables of Jesus seek to use—insofar as they are able—the tools of biblical research in their own probings.

(Spring) DCO takes on the Du Page County Treasurer for his alleged receiving of large unsecured loans from a number of area banks. He is indicted by a grand jury and comes under fire from his own party. DCO gains a measure of community respect as a watch-group where the issues are local, specific, and manageable.

(Summer) An important 60-page "Family Book" details CCS educational patterns and opportunities.

(Fall) Interest in educational opportunities mounts as issues seem ever more slippery all across the nation. Where one takes seriously the issues which may actually be changed by local people taking local initiative, the "Christ incognito" role, when localized, seems almost too confrontational and too scary.

(Fall) The Fifth Annual Workshop in Parish Renewal helps us to realize not only that things do not remain "as they were," but that the gifts of the Spirit also become new with the inevitability of change.

(Fall) Four theological students come, like two other groups before them, for two years of common ministry at CCS, a seminary-designated "teaching parish."

(Winter, 1977) We again face the pain of having fellow members whom we know and love move away to other cities and states. When you become "one in the Spirit," good-bye parties are a wrenching experience.

(Mar.) With the start of a Track III biblical interpretation group, over half the CCS adults are now into Scripture studies.

(Spring) New opportunities develop for working in tandem with the growing number of women pastors in such pursuits as "women in worship" seminars and workshops. We are becoming more inclusive not just in language and deeds, but also in feelings.

(Oct.) The sixth annual Pastors' Workshop seeks deeper caring in relation to problems of personal (even physical) renewal of clergy and laity.

(Fall) Workshops galore—on renewal, on women and worship, a "singular" workshop, and a number of one-day events on a great variety of issues.

(Winter, 1978) With projected growth in numbers, we attend to empathetic programs of integration and "ownership" of lay ministries.

(Winter) Community organization advances to a new level of broadly based west suburban supportiveness touching nearly every issue of citizen concern.

(Spring) The CCS Ministry to Musicians projects plans for foundation grants to jazz composers to create a whole new option in American hymnody, that of the American hymn based upon this country's unique gift to the world of art, jazz.

(Summer) Retreat, reflection, and planning for the third year of our new three-year curriculum designed for use in the Christian home.

(Summer) At a preconfirmation retreat teens get heavily into biblical interpretation, spending the better part of two days learning how to "think like a Hebrew."

(Fall) We plan to utilize a grant for awarding gifts to

artists who compose, create, paint, write, sculpt, or otherwise envision new artistic options for the contemporary church. Artists and theologians exchange ideas, expectations, and insights into the nature and interconnecting of their respective disciplines.

(1979) More than a decade along on our journey, we think big—of inviting world-renowned theologians to live within our Community for, say, a month or two, with the freedom to relate to their surroundings in whatever way they wish and with a commitment to be resourcefully "in-residence" for occasional preaching or teaching at CCS; of coming to grips with the meaning of the Last Supper for our regular eucharistic life; of our Ministry to Musicians bringing to Jazz Vespers some of the great names in American jazz; of adding full-time staff for enhanced ministry in arts and media, or in adult education, or in pastoral care and counseling; and of confronting again and again our fear of change and of the questions the 1980s must inevitably thrust upon the church that is open to God's future.

1. The Biblical Mandate: A Theology for Change

> Now the Lord said to Abram, "Go from your country and your kindred and your father's house to the land that I will show you. And I will make of you a great nation, and I will bless you, and make your name great, so that you will be a blessing."
> —Genesis 12:1,2

> Throughout all their journeys, whenever the cloud was taken up from over the tabernacle, the people of Israel would go onward. —Exodus 40:36

> You have heard that it was said to the men of old ... but I say to you ...
> —formula Jesus used six times in Matthew 5

> One thing I do, forgetting what lies behind and straining forward to what lies ahead ...
> —Philippians 3:13

Even a scanning of the Prologue's sketchy history of the Community of Christ the Servant will show how the raising of biblical-theological-historical questions helped continually to shape and reshape our exciting and surprise-filled ministry together. Those very questions provide us with certain theological models.

THE BIBLICAL CASE FOR CHANGE

Quite a long and serious case for flexibility, indeed for change, can be made from the biblical point of view. Biblical inquiry itself can show us how our individual and parish

26

lives may be freed from the "traditional" view of change as an enemy to sane and solid Christian existence.

It is even possible for us to understand the Old and New Testament stories and their chief characters and sagas as mandating change. From Abraham's experience with a God who seemed to act out his will *in front of* Abraham, leading him into unknown lands and adventures, to the kind of ultimate change Paul spoke of when he said, "Lo! I tell you a mystery, we shall not all sleep, but we shall all be changed, in a moment, in the twinkling of an eye, at the last trumpet" (1 Cor. 15:51,52), we get the impression that biblical characters understood change and an open and flexible future as being of and from God.

It is only fair and right that at this early point in the argument for change I declare myself as a full-fledged, un-ashamed radical-in-the-faith, that is, as one of tradition, of roots which run ancient and deep and which upon occasion also run countergrain to what we usually get away with in our popular labeling of "tradition," some of it not getting beyond what was good enough for grandma! A radical tra-ditionalist, stated John A. T. Robinson upon many occa-sions, is one who continually goes to his roots not only for perception but also for the freedom to move on. Without such roots one is unlikely to know deeply, and therefore have the security required of the religious person to ques-tion to the depths. Robinson also defined the "reformist" and the "revolutionary" in contrast to the "radical" who is always persistent in asking what roots are for! The reformist holds to tradition and seeks to update it, while the revolu-tionary regards tradition as essentially irreformable and is quite prepared, in most instances, to act outside tradition. The radical, on the other hand, never ceases to dig for roots through a mind which probes and which also uses the dia-logical constructs which help sharpen the live options in parish and personal life.

Contemporary Christians who yearn for the church to re-cover roots for the sake of growth will have to come to grips with certain biblical ambiguities. We may even have to deal with contrasting biblical and theological pictures, not simply choosing one over the other but taking them into our systems as models which we might hold in tension.

For example, Moses has become historically identified with the giving of the Law, almost to the exclusion of his role as deliverer of Israel from bondage. How has such a selected viewpoint become the modern mind-set? It has happened, in part, through our educational system, specifically through the catechizing process inflicted on millions of youngsters in most churches. Moses has thus become lawgiver, even the stern interpreter of a God whose chief wish for humanity is holding the line, living the restrictive life. Whatever part of that is indeed true-to-life in the remembrance of the reader, I am sure that it will be agreed that such a narrow accounting of the life of Moses is undeserved. My own remembrance of my initial encounter with the first part of Luther's catechism is one of thinking that the church has made it possible for me to understand the most important truths of the Bible in concise form; hence, law gets reduced to Decalogue, Moses becomes the historic symbol of law receiver/dispenser, and we begin to build personal and corporate life-styles which, in being legalistic, are biblically and theologically myopic.

The historic context is important in searching for biblical/theological roots. Moses' story is a tale deeply rooted in the Hebrew concept of God as *mover*. The God of the Exodus is the God of a semi-nomadic people, and one who moves not only *with* the people but *before* them, sometimes against the gods of the Canaanites and other times into new settings and new possibilities awaiting the covenant people. Moses is clearly identified as deliverer, leader of exodus, freedom fighter. In community organization terms, Moses was the prime organizer and the one who was to articulate "the issue" for God's people. It is important for the church to see and understand such a context in order to realize the pervasive relationship between concepts of God on the one hand and the idea of change on the other.

A CRISIS IN UNDERSTANDING

Despite the Biblical evidence, there is still today a crisis in faith and in interpretation for many Christians between a God of the past and a God for the future. Put another way, and with particular emphasis upon how local congregations see their ministries and tasks, there is a rather well-defined division between those Christians who prefer to see biblical systems as providing rigid, so-called orthodox views toward life, and those, usually in the minority, who experience religion not so much in terms of systems but in terms of open-ended, question-raising, often contradiction-laden frustrations.

The systematic approach by its very nature is attractive to men and women of any age, especially if there is a real desire to communicate the heritage, to teach the faith, to find some "handles," to relate truths to adults and children within clearly defined categories. It is difficult enough to invite people into a faith which they may ultimately "own" (have control over, feel good about, be able to articulate, give direction to) without complicating matters by avoiding comfortable systems. The church had long known that an effective approach to the teaching of religious history and to faith-concepts is that which is basically answer-oriented, related to the past, intellectually satisfying whenever possible, and often expressed through repeatable formulas, especially in tightly woven liturgies.

By contrast, the open or future-oriented approach to conveying biblical history and faith-concepts exhibits deep question-raising, an often highly developed eschatology, the feeling that risk—though it implies mistake-making—is part of the freedom which faith should hold to under the mercies of a God who wishes us to transform and reconcile all of life.

THE SYSTEMATIC/OPEN DIALECTIC

Both points of view, the systematic and the open, can be biblically substantiated. The two should be held in tension. The absolutizing of either one causes innumerable problems for the church and its view of its life and mission. More pointedly, a dialectical tension helps us deal with a current dilemma that really troubles church people: how to hold to a God who was more alive and active "back then" in "biblical times" before they closed the canon forever leaving us with the impression that God has no more will left in him to be dramatically portrayed in our age, no more surprises, no more exodus, no more tomorrows into which *we* might be invited. No wonder the good news has become stale and stuffy for millions of Christians in the western world. We have forgotten those biblical images of hope, of a transformed and renewed world, of the prophetic call to repent (turn around and *go* in a *new* direction). We are therefore condemned to telling each other of a good news which can never be contemporized because we have no God available to call our own generation into both action (risk) and expectation.

We have erred on the side of holding to the God of the status quo. Are we afraid of exposing the God of risk and change? Seldom have I found Christians devoid of either the will or the expertise to reach into biblical history and to be able to pull from it meanings and symbols. What I have found in the churches is considerable fright concerning change, reluctance to see change in any way related to biblical history, God, or a description of his will (unless as a will appropriate for people who lived in biblical days), and a near frantic grip on Scripture as a last bastion of law, order, and rationale which spells out the secure life in God from beginning to end. I'm afraid that the old bulletin board slogan about the church preaching and teaching a "changeless Christ for a changing world" still holds true for many a Christian.

The stress in much Christian thought upon a God who is antithetical to change can be tremendously dysfunctional in all aspects of parish self-undertanding and life. Church management, stewardship, evangelism, preaching, teaching, programming, social ministry, and liturgy all surely reflect whatever we believe our "textbook" understanding of God may be.

THE PROPHETS AND CHANGE

The Hebrew remembered the past while envisioning a future with new possibilities because he placed the Presence and the acts of God in that which goes *before* him and provides him with a sense of renewal and release. This view is rooted in the prophetic meaning of repentance. The prophet called for Israel to change her *ways,* not simply to feel sorrow over past actions or inactions. The prophets (in contrast to parts of Psalms and elsewhere) cared little about how sorrowful the feeling was, but insisted upon real and concrete action—turning around in direction! Amos described the "noise of solemn assemblies" as pious worship which substituted for real change. Dealing with the tensions between simply feeling sorrow and actually changing one's life-style can seriously affect both content and meaning in liturgy as well as in our specific social actions. We may certainly hold up in prayer and litany, in sermon and intercession, the sharp issues of racism, war, and corruption in local politics. The prophets call us to more, and tell us that it is not enough to be sorry that we are racists, or that we are at war, or that—too bad—we have elected those whom we have elected, and we are only a tiny voice without consequence. If we hear the prophets clearly then we hear them call us actually to *change* even while we *pray* for change. That is frighteningly direct and terribly radical as an intentional life-style. No wonder we rationalize and avoid dealing with the tension.

JESUS' MINISTRY

The dynamic living and moving God of our future (as well as our past) opens the future to us nowhere more movingly than in the New Testament and through the rabbinic teachings of Jesus. Even as Jesus repeatedly spoke his well-known ". . . but I say unto you," and attempted to lead the people beyond simplistic law fulfillment through his radicalizing of the law itself, he found almost instant responses of reluctance, confusion, and criticism. How dare this man, this carpenter's son, reinterpret, improve upon, or especially, go beyond the ancient law? Jesus had no argument with the law as guide to living in relation, but he knew that it could and had become a stumbling block which acted as an inferior substitute for a relationship between God and human beings. Since his message was one of relationship born in his Father's love for all humans and couched in hope, he challenged their right to absolutize the law, to make it a thing unto itself. Already by Jesus' day—in fact long before his day, as the prophets knew—ideas of truth, God, life, and servanthood in the name of God were becoming remembered words more than expectant events.

Jesus was more "Hebrew" than any of his contemporaries, especially those who took pride in their keeping of the law. His entire ministry was caught up in hope and future. Let me say it again: from first to last, and not merely in the epilogue, Christianity *is* eschatology, *is* hope, forward looking and forward moving, and this is why Jesus' followers are always revitalizing, refreshing, and transforming the present. Hope is not one element of Christianity but is the medium of Christian faith and the key in which everything is set.

At the very least Jesus apparently believed himself to be an authentic prophet. His self-consciousness might very well have developed all the way to—or, as some would argue, even have begun with—believing himself to be Son of God, Son of Man, Savior. My purpose is not to review the arguments pertaining to his self-consciousness, but to point to his prophetic self-understanding. His gospel was preached to outcasts. His quarrel was with rigid pharisaism. His involvement was with the common people, the tax collectors, prostitutes, and nonreligious. He made no attempt to coerce people into conversion as we sometimes experience it today. He was not a man of coercion. His rabbinic style allowed the questioner space and means to receive the question back again in order to "own it," as it were, and along with it a possible resolution or answer. Jesus seemed to enjoy his encounters with people; he was a good listener. His lifestyle in Matthew's Gospel is sharply contrasted with that of John the Baptist: Jesus is described as a glutton and wine bibber, one who circumvents the laws. Here was a man who provided a lively challenge to an encrusted form of Judaism, for no matter what the people had heard and held to "of old" —which included laws to keep them from breaking The Laws—he had the audacity to utter: ". . . but *I* say to you."

His message revealed a sensitivity that refused to reject the outcast, the failure, or even the irreligious. Slowly we learn to appropriate this radical message. For example, it was once commonly assumed that wounded soldiers were left to die on the battlefield. Only by the time of the Crimean war and with the daring of Florence Nightingale was there a risky decision made that the outcast, the wounded, must be rescued and treated. It was not until a century ago that epileptics were treated in any way other than that of the outcast. Only as people have begun to concern themselves with lepers, juvenile delinquents, the elderly, or the mentally or emotionally disturbed, have *we* then begun to see how radical movments—movements with God calling us into a more gracious and open future—have emerged.

THE OPEN FUTURE

The biblical roots concerning love call for the breaking out of oneself and entering arenas of empathy and servanthood. God calls us out of ourselves, out of our churches, out of whatever may tend to encase us or provide us with a lulling sense of "blessed assurance." As a matter of fact, assurances about the faith, about living the Christian life, are clearly not the only biblical points and liturgies to be heard.

Love and Liturgy

On the performance level of love, we seem to settle for so little so quickly. What we euphemistically refer to as justice is probably enlightened self-interest at best. Only occasionally do we find radical examples of biblical love in public arenas. Martin Luther King Jr. risked a portrayal of unarmed love and so created, as did "outsiders" to the faith such as Gandhi, significant change in attitude and in style of life for a whole nation if not the entire world. Unarmed love, undergirded by a theology for change and resulting in a clear congregational self-understanding, can become a creative dynamic in the face of the continuing challenge to the church by forbidding powers and principalities of the status quo. A liturgy which helps to articulate that theology and which is used regularly by the Community of Christ the Servant calls upon the people to pray as follows:

Leader: We may have the gifts of scientific prediction
    and understand the behavior of molecules,
    We may break into the storehouses of nature
    and bring forth new insights;
People: But devoid of love,
    all these mean nothing, O Lord!
Leader: We may give our goods
    to feed the poor;
    We may bestow gifts
    to charity;
People: But devoid of love,
    all these mean nothing, O Lord!
Leader: We may die the death of a martyr
    and spill our blood as a symbol
    of honor for generations unborn;
People: But devoid of love,
    all these mean nothing, O Lord!

Leader: O God, may we also see
how we might become self-centered in our
self-denial
and self-righteous in our self-sacrifice;
how our generosity may feed our ego,
and our piety our pride.
People: Without love, benevolence becomes egotism
and martyrdom becomes spiritual pride.
Leader: Yet the greatest of all virtues is love.
People: In a world dependent upon force and coercive
tyranny and bloody violence,
We are challenged by your loving Son
to follow in his love,
Leader: And to discover for ourselves
that unarmed love is the most powerful force in
the world.
People: Amen. So may it be.[1]

God's People and the Open Future

What does it mean to come to grips with being the people of God in this generation? What does it mean to come to grips with the God who has enriched our past, provided us with roots, guidelines for living, answers, mystery mingled in sacraments which hold us together, and stories and events which have no easy resolution or rigid interpretation? What does it mean to hold in tension with all that has been received from our illustrious past the many rich gifts yet to come: from graces from a God yet to be heard to new questions of justice, truth, and love, to the abrogation of simplistic law-keeping and to receiving the call to live—ever attentive both to past roots and to the Presence of the Spirit this day—as the church with an open future?

The traditional structuring of the church is that of a people with unanimity of views concerning God and the carrying on of its own tradition. Most of us have been

1. Jack Lundin, *Liturgies for Life* (Downers Grove: CCS Publishing House, 1972) , pp. 82–84.

"born into" a style of Christianity. Others have been attracted to that style of Christian life which is either attentive to their everyday emotional and spiritual needs or holds to the kinds of truths which make "common sense." We also tend to develop cultural systems and structures alongside the theological settings, and even geographic identities which heighten either the "closed" or "open" stance of the parish which lives within those communities. Finally, we practice, wittingly and unwittingly, what is often called civil religion.[2] We find in many of these settings fairly well-established and well-protected ghetto mentalities, exercising well-reasoned and usually well-programmed responses to who the members believe they are as the people of God in that particular spot. To say that this situation, including all of the varied components of civil religion, should be labeled as bad is to miss the point. Openness to the future means receptivity to one's roots, history, identity, and selfhood, *and* to those who call us into question or jostle our safe opinions, to the new or intruding thought or cause, the person who might interrupt our neatly arranged future. Elizabeth O'Connor in her well known book on the innovative Church of the Savior, Washington, D.C., put the tension well when she said, "If engagement with ourselves does not push back horizons so that we see neighbors we did not see before, then we need to examine the appointment kept with self."[3] Again, lest the point be missed: it is a matter of keeping past and present, system and openness, law and gospel, in creative tension.

Catholicity and the Open Future

Catholicity suggests diversity. Diversity within the parish often results in tension between programs as well as between people and ideas. Yet should it not be so? Paul described

2. See Robert Benne and Philip Hefner's treatment of American civil religion, *Defining America: A Christian Critique of the American Dream* (Philadelphia: Fortress Press, 1974) .

3. Elizabeth O'Connor, *Journey Inward, Journey Outward* (New York: Harper & Row, 1968) , p. 28.

the church as having various body functions. We are not all toes, or all arms, or all mouths, but work with respect and even harmony with each other. We therefore hurt when another part of the body hurts. We acknowledge the actions of the fingers even though we might prefer being the mind or the feet. We expect—or better, allow—such diversity to exist between parish and parish, between denomination and denomination, but seldom if ever *within* the local parish or denomination. To be sure, it can be pointed out that the denomination demonstrates more in the way of diversity in style and program than does the local parish. But each in its own way gives the impression to the world that particularity is the more attractive option, not universality.

The church ought to be equipped and able—even in local parish situations—to discard truths which no longer serve, maintain some old ways, learn how to make use of new insights into the truths available, and generally learn to touch and be touched by the gifts of others.

The New Adult for the Open Future

How shall the mandate for change and openness be received by the contemporary adult? A word must be spoken concerning the recipient of a theology of change and of dialectic. Albert van den Heuvel speaks of the "new adult":

> Little has been done about describing the new adult. He will be the man whom Kierkegaard tried to paint in his essay on the Knight of Faith (although few living people will ever arrive at such emotional stability) ; he will be the man whom Bonhoeffer called the man come of age. The dominant traits of his character will be flexibility rather than stability, trustworthiness rather than predictability, curiosity rather than knowledge, an experimental attitude rather than certainty, meditation rather than preaching, listening rather than proclaiming.[4]

4. Albert H. van den Heuvel, ed., *The New Creation and the New Generation* (New York: Friendship Press, 1965) , p. 70. Also on the subject of the contemporary adult, Clarence Kemp, "Changes in Patterns of Personal Values in

The new adult will be seen as a risk taker, aware of human foibles, empathetic and willing to become open to the future, open to hope, to other people and their ideas. Van den Heuvel adds the following prognosis for the new adult:

> He will need to be a man of choice in order to remain a person. His judgment will come tentatively and slowly because of his humor and relativism. His discipline may be strict but he will have no time for morality or absolute judgments. He will think inductively rather than deductively. The new adult will live on the road rather than in a house, and his decisions will come after discussions with many partners rather than after solitary reflection. Most of his commitments will be short term with a definite goal. He will search continuously, again and again rethinking his approach to people.
>
> In other words, he will look very much like the adolescent, the difference lies in the few long-term commitments he will make and the responsibility he will bear. But the outlook on life, the questions he faces, the changes he has to make in his thinking and actions will be the same as those of his younger partners in life.[5]

The Christian church already has sunk deep roots into a theology for change. Her Lord and Savior Jesus Christ was, in his brief and electric ministry, the chief harbinger of change. He comes into our world to give us the future, to call upon us to find him in it, freeing us by his grace as we go.

Relation to Open-Closed Belief Systems," *Christian Century* (March 1964), p. 75, says, "It becomes increasingly clear that the highly dogmatic individual is *less* likely to live the more creative individualized life of the one less hampered by the effects of dogmatism."

5. Van den Heuvel, *The New Creation*, p. 70.

2. Insider-Outsider:
The Church's Self-Understanding

At this time the disciples came to Jesus and said,
"Who is the greatest in the kingdom of heaven?" So
he called a little child to him and set the child in
front of them. Then he said, "I tell you solemnly,
unless you change and become like little children
you will never enter the kingdom of heaven. And so,
the one who makes himself as little as this little child
is the greatest in the kingdom of heaven."
—Matthew 18:1–4 (JB)

Finding himself cured, one of them turned back
praising God at the top of his voice and threw himself
at the feet of Jesus and thanked him. The man was a
Samaritan. This made Jesus say, "Were not all ten
made clean? The other nine, where are they? It
seems that no one has come back to give praise to
God, except this foreigner."   —Luke 17:15–18 (JB)

But a Samaritan traveler who came upon him was
moved with compassion when he saw him.
—Luke 10:33 (JB)

THE CHURCH'S SELF-UNDERSTANDING

The church's self-understanding is obviously conditioned,
tempered, slanted—even *fixed*—by how the church understands and tells the story, the gospel, the written and felt
relationship between a gracious God and human beings who
are free to interpret God's grace in often terrorizingly narrow ways. Many parishes today exist with a clearly discern-

ible aura of "worthy insider" about them—and that is no surprise. Denominationalism and local identity aside, one may ask, without any apology to Christian history, what kind of atmosphere *can* the church create when she conveys messages through words such as "save," "win for Christ," or even the phrase "to church people"? Ancient symbols for the church include that of the ship or boat and the image of someone throwing out the "lifeline" to the drowning sinner and of rescue from the cruel seas of life. These have permeated parish life for years and seem clearly to convey both that which is true and significant and also that which has given the church its self-understanding, albeit somewhat fraught with insider implications.

At the same time, the story we tell, indeed, the story we *are* and live out, is more complex.

Forced though we may be to deal with options, complexities, and discrepancies we would rather not face within the larger biblical story, we must avoid reducing the gospel to simplicities or slogans. We must keep from unnecessary absolutizing, from setting the story in concrete. We must also come to learn how to deal more sensitively with interpersonal relations, with ecclesiastical structures, and with a stronger, more holistic picture of God and his will for us humans.

For every picture of Moses catechetically reduced to a pose with law tablets, we also have the image of Abraham with a God yet to be shaped, and of promises and risks yet to be lived out. For every Psalm 1's insistence upon meditating upon the law, we find a quixotic and tenuous Psalm 22.

For every Bildad and Zophar and Eliphaz railing (in tones of true friendship, of course) against those who deserve God's punishment, we find a feisty Job standing firm in the face of a God who would deny Job neither his integrity nor his anger.

For every closed system of neatly packaged stories which one by one pretend to unveil the mysteries of God's will, there are the words and images which are invitations for us to celebrate a God and his grace which himself and itself are continually *becoming!*

One does not need to insist upon discovering such options in all biblical themes. One accepts them wherever found, and like Jacob who sought a deeper and more definitive self-understanding, begins to wrestle with the angel, to grow, to discover, to define a personal destiny.

All this is said in order to help us slip quietly into the very touchy arena of contemporary congregational life and specifically of an insider mentality which seems so prevalent in parish life. As one pastor told me, "If we've got the product to sell and people need that product, then why be wishy-washy about the insider-outsider thing. Let's without shame be God's insiders with good news and salvation on our lips." Though I might appreciate his enthusiasm, I certainly would wish to parry and joust with him over some of his consumer images. Yet I think we would all agree that there is considerably more—more depth, more sensitivity— to uncover as we define who we are as uniquely Christian. The story of evangelism, and of becoming "fishers of men," and of understanding that unique command which is the church's to "go into all the world and make disciples," has its history, its context, its larger story which we need to keep hearing lest we slip off of the line of tension between the role of insider-outsider in religious life.

THE CHURCH AND THE OUTSIDER

The long and glorious story of the church's growth—and here I mean mostly numerical—has to be understood in the light of the concomitant scars and blemishes which have occurred when humans even unintentionally assume an insider attitude in the proclamation of the gospel. Some scars were formed in various ages in the life of the church whenever zeal on the evangelist's part coerced or bullied people into the warmth of the fold. Church history is sprinkled with such stories as that of Charlemagne or Charles the

Great (A.D. 800). To be a subject of Charles meant to be a Christian, at least in name. His decree that all children must be baptized in their first year and that all people must go to church on Sundays and feast days would not be very popular in countries where the freedom of religion includes the privilege of saying a stout "No!" The history of religious institutions, particularly the church, records embarrassing failures of the church to respond whenever humanly possible to the fullest exposition of the gospel concerning evangelization of the world. That gospel understanding must take seriously the attitude of Jesus of Nazareth as to who insiders and outsiders might be and how they were treated during his own brief ministry.

Who are the outsiders for Jesus? Did he call them or invite them to become insiders? Were the trips Jesus made at the very beginning of his ministry into gentile country for the purpose of declaring that the mission of the church after the resurrection might be for the whole world? "If we reject the idea of a mission to the Gentiles as the purpose of Jesus' ministry, we are forced to rethink the question of the reason why Christianity burst the bonds of Judaism."[1] In the mission and message of Jesus *is it not the place of the outsider*—Gentile or dispossessed—*which is paramount?* Here is a crucial question for the contemporary parish as it teaches people assumptions concerning the church's self-understanding and how that self-understanding is made known within the neighborhood. From such assumptions, such mind-sets, we develop unique and identifiable styles of life. Parish identity ought not be tainted with exclusivism or with the careless set of insider attitudes which might then appear to the surrounding community as sheer snobbery or at least a kind of self-sufficiency.

The tension between the roles of the insider and the outsider for Jesus precludes the church's acting in self-sufficient ways.

1. David Granskou, "Christology" (Lecture delivered at the Community of Christ the Servant, Lombard, Ill., September 12, 1968).

The question we all need to address again and again is does not the outsider *also* call the insider to repentance? Was it not the outsider, the Samaritan, the leper who in an embarrassing number of instances in the Gospel records becomes the true evangelist?

The Good Samaritan in Luke 10 is clearly a story of insider-outsider, *not* a story of neighborliness or a dictum to always stop for distraught hitchhikers.

Among the ten lepers in Luke 17 there was but one who returned to give thanks for healing. He was an embarrassment, and had he not been identified as the one outside the religious fold of Israel acting in responsive thanksgiving, ears would not have stung and the story itself would either not have been told or would have been redundant. It was and is a story of tension between people who *know* what to do and how to give thanks because of their relationship— their insider identity—but *do* not! And of one who instinctively and without the wraps of such religious stability still acted out of gratitude, thus genuinely responding to the grace of God.

Even the lovely legend of the magi in Matthew 2 becomes an interesting study as outsiders act out the roles of sources of wisdom, healing, and openness, and thus some of the dimensions of grace.

For the church to play out the roles of exclusivity, of protectiveness, of fear of learning and listening to how God's grace is active in the outside world, is for the church to abdicate its distinctive role of being the church.

How humbling that we church people must also look to those who live so sensitively yet who are outside our walls and who may from time to time come to see us as rather pompously proclamatory and even recalcitrant. The very word "preach" has become in the popular mind "don't you preach to me," and even "sermon" is many times seen as that long, boring time when I am "preached to."

To take ourselves so seriously is not only to forfeit our sense of perspective on who we are in God's kingdom and

purpose, but to completely forget that we are the earthen-
ware vessels which need, especially when we become
"cracked," to be broken to bits, watered liberally, and
slapped back on the potter's wheel for reshaping and reuse
among all who figure in God's vast plan. Exclusivity simply
doesn't suit the church of Jesus Christ! An acknowledged
vulnerability, which will help us in our evangelism to listen
as well as proclaim, does!

Sociological factors have also contributed to both public
and church sanction of the insider mentality. We have places,
more properly, institutions, for the feeble-minded, the epi-
leptic, the disturbed, and the criminal. We even have
sanctuaries for the creative and innovative in our society.
Any of us who have come to know those called "deviate"
know that such persons live in a special kind of anguish
which separates them from "normal" people, and quite often
no amount of talk, defense, or explanation can assuage the
labeling which tells everyone that they are people who, for
whatever reason, are outsiders!

The sick, the leper, the outcast were not cast away, con-
fined, or categorized by Jesus. At the same time, Jesus did
not allow the religious insider any sense of privilege by virtue of some exclusive stance as practicing believer. Being
called-out Children of the Covenant was never meant to become a wedge between people—even accidentally. Rather,
for many Old Testament characters, and certainly for the
story line, it was a means of offering clear identity as a covenant people. For Jesus' disciples and the early church, identified through his radical love and acceptance, it caused
Christians to also accept an open life, wisdom from the outside, and an awareness of the need to break down the barriers
which society set up to separate people from each other.

Had the church kept a radical insider-outsider tension and
teaching clearly visible we might not have nurtured so easily
the common attitude which many a non-Christian holds
toward the church: that of exploiter of people's lives and

earnings for highly dubious purposes of self-aggrandizement and vested interest. Our critics do not hold such views without some validity. We, the church, are indeed late entries into the crucial ministries of reconciliation amidst the racial, economic, and sociopolitical struggles of our day. Intramural parish-oriented programming calls for large investments of time and money, often without significantly touching the lives of others beyond the parish. Even budget monies dedicated to benevolence and welfare are given with a sense of frustrating anonymity.

How then does one deal with "insidism" in the parish? Is it a disease peculiar to people who have been called "peculiar" and who are glad, even relieved and joyous, over being separated, won, committed, called-out and set apart?

How also can one refuse to be impressed by the contemporary "know how" in evangelism, by zesty churchmanship filled with offers the laity dare not turn down? Does this questioning not also suggest the possibility of a tortuous kind of turnaround in parish mind-set and life-style? As I look back upon the years of just such questioning in the Community of Christ the Servant I recognize that any congregation bold enough to call itself "an experimental expression" of the church is already in for big and dangerous assumptions of exclusivity!

RAISING NEW QUESTIONS

There was immediate cause, at CCS, to acknowledge a different style of witness simply because we were not to be a territorially organized mission congregation. Parish, as a term, usually means geographic region. We were not a parish in that sense. We couldn't send out teams according to Luke 10, two by two, even if we wanted to. We were extra-territorial, nongeographic or, as some preferred, an alternative style congregation. And further, it was part of our task to give over time and energy to the very questions

of our identity, our theological underpinnings, our life together in defined, defended, and directed words about word
and sacrament.

New christological questions began to prompt new expressions of the Christian life and witness. As to the insider-
outsider images, we had to square with a view which many
of the very first members of CCS called "both and!" That
is, we were unashamedly *called-out* and *radically separated*
by a grace which has its own tug, pull, and warmth within
the insider Christian setting. On the other hand, we were
determined also to be "of the outside," in a kind of tension
with the church as establishment or human institution, cau-
tioning each other that such institutions have great and
nearly irresistible temptations to take themselves much more
seriously than they (we!) ought. The tension is not an easy
one to live with, and we have often fallen to one side or the
other—too protected or too rejecting. Yet as we began to
count the ways the outsider was demonstrating the compassion of Christ, labels began getting all mixed-up and our
concept of the expansiveness of grace kept on festering and
enlarging.

From Mind-Set to Life-Style

At first we found that our refusal to routinely develop
pledge cards, wear lapel buttons, assign official greeters, make
financial calls, organize and train evangelism teams, and
even talk about money needs independently of the issues
people could genuinely *own*, all caused us to actually develop an alternative program or style nearly by default.

The first year or so was like living somewhere between
programmed questioning of programs and sheer fright.
What kind of *qualitative* growth might a church seek out?
How does personal faith (cultic expressions, piety, biblical
insights, and human support) juxtapose with corporate
servanthood (the call to serve others' needs, political stance,
risk, and real action for the sake of change within sociopolitical systems)?

How does one listen compassionately to the person who demands more than planned-out, compartmentalized, and highly organized programs from the church? And how does one empathize, touch base with, and invite *into* that quizzical structure called parish that same person—hurts, expectations, hopes, and all—without simply developing *another* system which, in time, will also manage to eat us all up? Shall we playfully yet intentionally discourage people from joining with us in a covenant involving expectations of our becoming a "Christ incognito" (see chap. 5)? Shall we at the same time invite them to participate in, enjoy, and struggle along with us—oblivious to insider/outsider distinctions, until such time, if ever, as there is indication of willingness, even eagerness to covenant? Might there then be a more evident and even full understanding of what radicality an "inside" relationship may actually define? What then does it mean to belong? Does not our very concern about belonging suggest that we might not be conveying to the world the best and deepest image of the evangel as noncoercive, and of the evangelist as a better listener than a talker, a vulnerable someone rather than simply a "faith flaunter"?

Getting It All Together?

There is something rather rancid which keeps inflicting itself on the church as well as the culture—a true contemporary action of Satan—an attitude which prompts otherwise astute, open, and caring humans to think that we have to somehow "get it all together!" Who are we to impress with such a stance? Certainly not God. He knows beyond a shadow of a doubt that not one among us has much of anything so together. God help us! We no sooner read the marching orders given to the creative minority of disciples, and the history which indicates how quickly the early Christians multiplied into a majority, even a power to be reckoned with, than we are tempted to make corporate coercive fools of ourselves and our witness while at the same time misread-

ing and misrepresenting the very grace which—in freedom—
we now use for promotion purposes.

My guess is that there are some people, at least, who want
the church to be just a little less sure, a little less authori-
tarian, a little less impressive in having it all together—lest
we lose the child in us,[2] lest that carefully concealed crack
in our selfhood keep out the continuing supply of God's
graceful surprises which keep us alive, listening, growing
or, horror of horrors for some—even *changing!* Or else we
must face the possibility that when we speak together of repentance, we really don't mean what those who wrote the
Bible meant when they used the word, that is, a joy which
often comes about through both pain and insight, mutually
given and received, which precipitates an act of change in
one's life. In fact, maybe the act actually comes before the
reflection upon it. Growing through pain which leads to
joy has occurred in us hundreds of times, even though the reluctance to encounter it is a normal human feeling.

Structural Implications

In the ministry of Jesus the living of the open life clearly
means a willingness to accept wisdom from both inside *and*
outside, cognizant that God often chooses the outsider as
vehicle for his grace especially when and if the insider makes
grace an exclusive gift. The implications of this openness
for congregational life and structure reside not so much in a
lessening of the concern for organization, or a continual
shifting from one structural posture to the next, but rather
in raising on a continuous basis the level of conscious awareness of the tension which is always present whenever ownership of such weighty thoughts becomes apparent.

There is no need to disband energetic evangelism committees or well-motivated stewardship groups, or to fear our
own witness even if it does become accidentally tainted with

2. John K. Boutrager, *Free the Child in You* (Philadelphia: Pilgrim Press,
1974). See especially Part II.

a coerciveness born of enthusiasm. But there is need to be reminded of and occasionally to find structural opportunities to articulate the mission and ministry of Jesus: how seriously he took people, how deeply he listened, how severely he criticized religion which would clean the outside of the cup but fail to clear out the inside first (Matthew 23). To do this is to keep in perspective a tension that the church, by her very nature and self-understanding, must learn to live with.

Further, and in a very descriptive sense, listening to insider/outsider tensions caused the CCS experiment to do some significant restructuring. We learned in our experience that those who live out the single life-style; that is, the divorced, widowed, those who are single parents, unmarried parents, parish members with non-member spouses, those who are separated, those who cohabitate, and the single-by-choice, all yearn for a sense of identity and compassion *within* the religious community. To separate into "singles" clubs, divorce-support groups, or parents-without-partners may be necessary simply to hold one's style in supportive perspective by one's peers. On the other hand it was also recognized that such a near division can isolate and protect. Family life can easily become enemy or envied; the single life can appear remote, romantic, and alluring to the out-of-touch person who moves only in family circles within the congregation. Worse, each may begin to justify *their* life-style as more identified with the *Christian* way of life simply by failing to live in tension with others within the congregation itself.

As a consequence of the questioning process and of holding up the christological implications of insider/outsider tensions, it was decided to allow for "separating" structures to develop within parish life for purposes of support (i.e. divorce support group) but to keep such structures open to people whose lives do not automatically "fit," either by circumstance or definition. We also decided to invite people into structural divisions as such not on the basis of *age* (the teens or senior citizens) or *sex* (women's groups or circles, men's clubs) or *relatedness* (couples' club, singles' groups) but rather by virtue of issues which may cause a teenager, a grandmother, a divorced person and a couple in marriage to find their lives interacting *in the pursuit of a cause,* an issue held in common interest.

As a result the structure of CCS looks considerably different than, say, that of some three other parish experiences which were mine over the past twenty years. In such normative experiences and in accordance with the constitution of the congregation, we organized, structured, and became functional by virtue of age, sex, pairings, and the internalized tasks of maintaining the system. Women's groups and youth groups abounded; stewardship and evangelism committees were set up alongside finance, education, and worship and music groupings and, according to parish size, location, needs, various special groupings of people, but rarely according to issues.

At CCS we made the constitutionalized provisions for the "standing" committees a permissive rubric rather than a mandatory one and proceeded to organize on the basis of issues with the perspectives of the insider/outsider as christological commentary.

Ministries have developed as a result, ministries already sketched and given brief description in the Prologue. There are ministries which people *own* because of their abiding interest in them: housing the offices of the American Civil Liberties Union and the County Mental Health Association; a Tuesday evening health club; a ministry to the disenfranchised and politically impotent American Indians living in greater Chicago; a ministry to freedom of the press (secular and religious); a liturgical deacons' group interested in learning more about the history of worship and in leading the people in authentic worship; seminars and/or workshops in cooperation with neighboring churches for singles, married, divorced; publishing experiments; ministry to area jazz musicians whose alienation from the church is well-known but whose sensitivity to God and his grace is both surprisingly open and sharp; community organization which will serve as a convening vehicle for people who are aware of political power and what it may do to the life of a community for good or ill; a Chilean refugee committee which began with a study of a denominational statement protesting governmental involvement in the coup of 1974 and ended up sponsoring a family exiled from Chile; ministries in media, film-making, camping, and hunger information; the Alliance to End Repression which works for poor and disenfranchised prisoners jailed without due process and without ombudsman; workshops for parish clergy and laity to share ideas, anguishes, roots, and hopes. All represent groping efforts of a church to *become afresh* God's people, set in tension with a world which can ill afford to separate and divide itself into comfortable, look-alike compartments.

3. Faults We Haven't Even Used Yet: The Church Therapeutic

> I can will what is right, but I cannot do it. For I do not do the good I want, but the evil I do not want is what I do.   —Romans 7:18–19

> We've got faults we haven't even used yet.   —Pogo

> And if I have prophetic powers, and understand all mysteries and all knowledge, and if I have all faith, so as to remove mountains, but have not love, I am nothing.   —1 Corinthians 13:2

ORDINARY—HEROIC TENSIONS

Pogo's brief ego-pinching quote, "We've got faults we haven't even used yet," hangs in the CCS Commons in crudely drawn technicolor.[1] Its prominence causes visitors to smile. Its impertinence insists upon our remembering another christological axiom and, like the tensions of open versus system and insider versus outsider, to reexamine how we must manage to live out of the interesting paradox noted by Martin Luther, that we, being human, are *simul justus et peccator*—simultaneously justified *and* sinner. Not either/ or, but both! Both at the same time. What a terribly unresolved definition of the human condition to have to live with, much less understand. Yet we—the justified and

---

1. The exact Pogo quote reads: "We have faults which we have hardly used yet." After a great deal of archival work Martin Marty discovered the discrepancy, but he urges us to retain the "CCS version" rather than repaint our walls.

the sinful—are the ones who "people" that perfect/imperfect community known as the church.

To be sure, the church can reduce itself to a mere self-serving institution and can act out a *peccator* instinct more imaginatively destructive than that of any emperor or tyrant. On the other hand, that same human group may, by the grace which acts itself out in ordinary people who dare such vulnerability, become a real manifestation of God's Kingdom at a given time and place.

But the "job description" for each is not what one might expect. Instead of a heroic role for the Christian intent on fulfilling God's will in service to others, it becomes apparent that the Gospels point to the opposite, namely, the non-heroic, or ordinary.

When the Christian life is continually spoken of in heroic terms, one gets the impression that a good faith performance involves heroic role-playing, consciously or, better, I suppose, unconsciously. Was not Jesus the hero of the faith, an example for all to follow? Do we not talk of the heroes of the Bible? Can any parish long exist in a competitive society without tooting its horn in some sophisticated or even blatant manner? Indeed, the Christian life is spoken of, especially programatically, in heroic terms.

Some of it is unavoidable. Our cultural expectations, our sociopolitical attitudes have already introduced us to the language of "total commitment," going the "extra mile," "self-denial," being "set apart," becoming an "example for your neighbor," or even "honk if you love Jesus!"

The more perfect the example, the more cohesively the fellowship holds together, and the more expressly defined the witness of the church's faith to the surrounding community! Or, so goes the rarely challenged mind-set.

But we must also deal with the tension Luther speaks of in his definition of man, the tension Paul acknowledges within himself when he mentions his frustrated intentions to "do the good," and the basic teaching of Jesus concerning the nature of the *human beings* making up his church!

Jesus knew and was repelled by the elitism within the religious establishment of his day. On the one hand, the Pharisee was a sincere exponent of the law and, contrary to the preaching which is tempted to make him out as simply rigid and without compassion, he dedicated his life to the living out of the laws of God. Jesus rankled and upset the Pharisees because he was bringing in a new order that was more than practicable law-keeping, a new sensitivity to and relation with both God and one's neighbor.

Note, for example, how Jesus and John the Baptist are contrasted in Matthew 11:12–18. John appears religiously more acceptable, living in the wilderness, preaching repentance, while Jesus seems to live to the fullest, proclaiming a kind of dispensation toward law by setting himself into the unacceptable context of persons of questionable reputation and example. His message was not repentance as such but forgiveness, joy, and new life. The question raised in Matthew is the extent to which this kind of message and behavior on the part of Jesus became offensive to those who held to the heroic religious mind-set. Was Jesus bent on an identity with the undesirables and if so, why? Should he not have set a better example, cajoled them to the performance level of the faith which would, in and of itself, identify them with being serious about their relationship with God and consistent in their worship words and their daily living?

Jesus was, in this sense, a devastation for the *religious* people. Their expectations, their heroic models, found no support in the historic Jesus of Nazareth. Why should the Son of Man risk a tainted reputation by keeping company with known sinners? Was this flaunting of the rules not reason enough for the religious leaders of the day to call him severely in question?

But even in the history of the church, we Christians have been tempted to separate ourselves from the sinner as if to buy time and space in which to act out, to live out the joys of "being in Christ"—and so gain in understanding, and in direct communion with him, the meaning of Life! The Qumran community, the monastic communities, pietism's various formations over the centuries, even today's "Jesus freaks" and the well-motivated and intentioned T-groups, prayer-circles, and charismatic meetings *may,* often quite *unintentionally,* cause us to lose sight of the invitation to live within the tension of the heroic-ordinary dimension of the faith.

THE ORDINARY STYLE

The "ordinary" style of Christian life means being fully attentive to one's vulnerabilities; being "saved" more for life in this world than in that which is to come beyond one's death; exhibiting joy and risk in the process of listening to others; being sensitive to sounds, to colors, to how all the creatures on earth live and move; being as aware as possible of time, and of one's own interchange with all of creation as a gift given and received.

Paul described Jesus as the Second Adam—a rather startling model. Jesus as new Adam (1 Cor. 15:45–46) is actually juxtaposed to the Adam which we are—to "mankind," as the Hebrew word *Adam* roughly translates. In this unique relationship between Christ and the human there are common properties. Jesus did not think to "snatch at equality with God" (Phil. 2:7, NEB) but rather made himself nothing— "ordinary"?!—assuming the role of a servant, so intent was Jesus to break down the wall which separates. He would abolish "in his flesh the law of commandments and ordinances, that he might create in himself one new man in place of the two, so making peace, and might reconcile us both to God in one body through the cross" (Eph. 2:15–16).

Jesus' Ordinariness

I am continually impressed in the synoptic Gospel accounts and in the theology of the Epistles, with the ordinariness of Jesus. He was nearly an incognito figure. In Jesus' own life, one reads the amusing and occasionally mysterious commentary that he "lost himself in the crowd," and one wonders how such a powerful person, so charismatic a character, could go about losing himself in a crowd which he, by his power of personality and speech, had just moments before aroused to livid anger or aggressive action or compassionate attentiveness.

Descriptions of Jesus' death in Matthew and Mark seem nonheroic over against the Lukan Passion account (Luke 23:24, 27–32, 40–43, 46). For Luke, Jesus dies with quiet assurance; in other Gospel accounts he dies—as Dave Granskou likes to say—"with a scream!" (see Mark 15:37; Matt. 27:50) Take your choice. For me, his ordinariness, his identity with *my* scream, is persuasive, notwithstanding the years of identity with the neatly packaged, well-planned, three-hour Good Friday services which I have attended and conducted.

A Word for Spontaneity

One of the most arresting of the biblical images depicting the ordinary as against the heroic, and also one of the most embarrassing for the heroic contemporary church comes out of Matthew 25:31–46. In the story of the final separation of the sheep and the goats, we quickly learn that it is not only the "righteous" who are surprised by the unexpected verdict. The "ordinary" too are surprised to find a vindication toward their identifying with and caring for "even the least of these" as having "done it" to God himself. So identified with human destiny, sufferings, joys, and trials is God that any separation—no matter how heroic for purposes of calling us to act out God's will—is intolerable. The ordinary responsiveness, the empathy, the attentiveness to one's fellow human is the conspicuous point of this authentic account of Jesus' ministry.

Is life then to be seen as a serendipitous affair? Are law and judgment to be thrown out? Of course not. The point is: appropriate tension between the inevitable lure of playing out the roles of evangelist, stewardship pacesetter, or righteous example and the often silent witness which simply listens to human anguish, rejoices "with those who rejoice" and weeps "with those who weep" (Rom. 12:14) demonstrates beyond the many pages of the annual parish report that life is *more* than strictures and structures, caring is *more* than moral and ethical purity, and responsiveness to the gospel is *more* than calculated and performed duty.

Love Incognito

One of the most familiar and also most beautiful biblical examples of the heroic-ordinary tension is Paul's incantation of nonheroic compassion in 1 Corinthians 13. Here Paul makes clear that the obvious religious virtues—witness, suffering for truth, faith, generosity—all may fit models of religious heroism. Yet it is in placing such attractive acts in tension with the ordinariness of love that we see the reflections necessary to living out the life in Christ! Suffering for truth, or for anything, for that matter, *can* become masochistic. Yet in ordinary love, the love that operates incognito, even such suffering may also be redeemed and rescued from self-serving.

There have been in Scripture, and continue to be in our history, people who have lived out a nonostentatious, servant-oriented, nonheroic life-style; some to a lesser degree than others, but all somehow "impressive" in and by their willingness to keep on *becoming*, and to do so in near-incognito manner. I think of Jeremiah, often called the magnificent failure, or the madman who bought his piece of downtown Jerusalem as a matter of trust in God while knowing that Nebuchadnezzar's army was even then pounding at the city gates—and he did it from a jail cell.

Or Paul, with his quixotic musings, his little "boasting" about being caught up "whether in the body or out" (2 Cor. 12:1–6), and what psychologists today would probably identify as his struggle to make vital touch with his uncontrollable unconscious and thus the mystery of our human vulnerability.

Or Luther, who is too often made into a hero but seemed nonetheless to perceive the necessity for theology to define, even underscore, the vacillation within the human in our temptations to play out the heroic and to apologize for the ordinary.

Or Bonhoeffer. Or Marx, Dostoevsky, Kierkegaard, and many others whose names are recognizable and whose lives are often described as being occasionally "mad," yet touching deeply the roots of human vulnerability

A MENTAL HEALTH MODEL

We need to speak clearly of human vulnerability. To know that vulnerability, without any flaunting of our immorality or failures, is "okay" might be helpful for today's parish. In a telling comment on our anxiety over the tensions of the heroic-ordinary Harold Haas sets forth a model which allows the congregation itself to become a therapeutic instrument. He contends that churches have a positive role to play in enhancing mental health among their members, even to the point of counteracting unfortunate experiences individuals may encounter at the hands of family, peers, or other social institutions.

> The New Testament concept of the local church is absolutely fascinating from a mental health point of view. The picture presented in the New Testament of God's saints meeting in one place as a church has, among other things, these three characteristics: (1) It is a confessing community. (2) It is a community in which the members do not judge one another. (3) It is a community in which the members forgive one another and then restore one another in the spirit of meekness. It is, in other words, a community in which individuals can dare to be open and frank about themselves and with one another. It is a community in which the individual ought to have no fear of being made to feel worthless, dirty, unlovable because of what he is.[2]

2. Harold I. Haas, *The Christian Encounters Mental Illness* (St. Louis: Concordia Publishing House, 1966), pp. 100–101.

The described church, Haas admits, is hard to find even in the world of parishes which nonetheless make the attempt to live in such therapeutic tensions and/or allowances. He says this is understandable in the light of human sinfulness.

> What is not so understandable is that churches seem not to care about or to be conscious of their *potential* for being such a therapeutic community. Often they are not making a deliberate effort to really work out the New Testament image of the church as a confessing, nonjudging, restoring community of believers.[3]

And even more to the point of our holding in tension the insider-outsider and the heroic-ordinary biblical models so deeply rooted in Jesus' own ministry, he says:

> In the church (therapeutic) the unloved child can . . . find people who care. Here the insecure adolescent can find people who accept him as he is, who do not ask whether he is a good athlete or makes high grades or drives a pink convertible before they will like him or show him regard. Here the ex-alcoholic, the controlled sex deviate, the convicted criminal can find acceptance without fear of rejection or humiliation. Here the middle-aged depressive can find useful volunteer employment and be brought the Word of God, not by a professional elite, the clergy, but by people who care . . . a therapeutic community.[4]

Living with these tensions may not be easy or automatic in the life of the religious community. But they need to be given attention, held up, and remembered as part of our deepest roots in the life, attitudes, ministry, and teachings of Jesus Christ.

What directions a local group of Christians should take in structuring basic Christian ministries and concerns is a difficult question. How can we best, and with sensitivity toward our own vulnerabilities and toward the judgments of others, become openly therapeutic and genuinely supportive of each

3. Ibid.
4. Ibid.

other? The persistent question may well defy the best laid parish planning. If we pay more attention to the process itself, more attention to each other as persons, our image vis à vis world, community, or the fellow in the next pew, will become its very own reward.

But to work with determination for those therapeutic times requires of a congregation utter dependency upon the Holy Spirit and an utter willingness to be open to other human beings. It can mean liberating change: being able both to laugh and to cry within the context of freeing and wholesome worship rather than having to stifle one's momentary amusement and, out of fear or shame of personal revelation, cover over one's need to weep when only tears will suffice. "Naming the name" is not so important for our identity as Christians as the quiet, empathetic, responsive touch we may both give and receive—the clearest evidence of our doing the Father's will.

4. Being Held Together: The Eucharistic and Eschatological Community

For I received from the Lord what I also delivered to you, that the Lord Jesus on the night when he was betrayed took bread . . . broke it . . . any one who eats and drinks without discerning the body eats and drinks judgment upon himself.

—1 Corinthians 11:23,24,29

He (Luther) was at one with the early church in agreeing that the fellowship of the Sacrament is determined by the Koinonia which is not an association of men but a *metalepsis,* a partaking of the body of Christ . . . not by the will of men . . . but by the body of Christ. —Werner Elert,
*Eucharist and Church Fellowship
in the First Four Centuries*

The worship of Christians is dominated by God's eschatological gift of salvation, and remains open to God's future acts. It concerns both the future that God ever gives anew to his community in this world and the expectation of the consummation.

—Ferdinand Hahn,
The Worship of the Early Church

THE INWARD JOURNEY

When Elizabeth O'Connor spoke of the "inward journey" and the "outward"[1] she was describing the twin function of

1. Elizabeth O'Connor, *Journey Inward, Journey Outward* (New York, Harper & Row, 1968).

61

parish life: the rhythm of receiving grace and returning it to life all around us in servanthood. One act does not necessarily precede the other. They are dynamic, not ordered, perceived by the poetry of theology and not by some clever systematic which either insists that grace activates response or that human action is ratified by grace. One might muse over whether we believe our way into acting or act our way into the discovery of belief. The former is usually touted, but the tension is important for the church's holistic educational understanding (dealt with in chapter 6).

For our purposes here, it will be structurally convenient for us to see the ebb and flow of the *inward* absorbing of grace; that is, of our delight to see how the unashamed sopping up of that grace is sharply and radically focused on worship. It will be helpful for us to deliberate upon the "means of grace," the sacrament in particular called Eucharist, the joyous, grace-filled thanksgiving carried out in and through a drama couched in mystery.

Christian worship is certainly many-faceted and its drama involves many actions and many people enacting the drama. It is remembered past; it is instruction and illumination for the present; and it is invitation and hope for the future. Of the three, however, the early church best understood and gave most attention to future, to hope, to all that is implied by the word "eschatology."

The worship of the first two centuries in particular was undergirded by the worshipers' attention and sensitivity to the eucharistic *event* and the eschatological *event*, and both were interwoven into a feeling which gave "the moment" life, vitality, and Presence, but which also provided for a view of future as that which was also imminent and filled to the brim with urgent expectations. That the Christian congregation at worship knew they were gathered to be fed and caused to scatter as an act of good news permeating the world is very evident. That the contemporary worship setting has lost significant touch with that era—with or without our romanticizing the "early church"—is also disturbingly evident.

There are those who wonder where joy has gone in our worship. Have we too quickly settled for rigid performance of liturgy as against spontaneous drama, for a cerebral understanding against a visceral appropriation, for propriety of form against a freedom to feel deeply, for a vertical relation to God against risky touching of another human being, for listening to the history once made by the saints against making history anew in the give and take of shared grace in dynamic worship?

> For the Church is the world's most talkative institution . . . these impoverished Christians do nothing in their religious observances except chatter. They tell God what he ought and ought not to do, and inform him of things of which he is already well aware, such as that they are miserable sinners, and proceed then to admonish one another to feel guilt and regret about abominable behavior which they have not the least intention of changing. If God were the sort of being most Christians suppose him to be, he would be beside himself with boredom listening to their whinings and flatteries, their redundant requests and admonitions, not to mention the asinine poems set to indifferent tunes which are solemnly addressed to him as hymns.

> This was why I was always attracted to the old style of Roman Catholicism, wherein you could steal into church unnoticed and listen to a perfectly unintelligible service in splendid Gregorian chant. The whole thing was music, and God was not bored.[2]

H. L. Mencken poked jabs at the puritan heritage when he said the American looks as if he is fearful that somewhere someone may be enjoying himself.

We have managed to manage, regularize, and contain "proper" worship until it no longer explodes out of the wellsprings of grace but merely delivers up all that might be expected out of the mind-set of controlled and controlling humans. The Christian church of our day suffers a paralysis in its worship life, that is, in its very essence.

2. Alan Watts, *In My Own Way* (New York: Pantheon Random House, 1972), pp. 48, 49.

REGAINING THE CELEBRATORY

One does not memorialize the church-in-convention to *do* something about its worship life, although even that might bespeak a corporate awareness that something is wrong. But *our* fixing it up is not where we must begin. Our *letting* something occur, our getting out of the way, so to speak, might be a more creative attempt to deal with a malady of our own making.

Again we are faced with an interesting tension. (If you are beginning to see—even feel—the necessity to go about the business of theology out of the perspective of the dialectic, then you are beginning to understand the peculiar *schema* or argument of this book.) We who would define the church as that people who are caught up by and in word and sacrament and who are also given the task to preach and interpret that same word and to administer the sacraments, are inextricably caught in the very tension (and thus the dialectic) between what is given by God and how the gift is received, understood, and made demonstrable in that unique arena called worship. How much inevitable control, adjustment or fitting—maybe even squeezing—into the human situation should be expected of that grace which chooses to pinpoint itself and its gifts in human lives? Is the sky the limit? Is there a certain madness about worship which, if we understand the scope and power of grace, must be at least felt as we prepare to enter the arena? And if it is true that "we've got faults we haven't even used yet," if our definition of the human is dialectically perceived as *simul justus et peccator* (simultaneously justified and sinner), then we can hardly avoid allowing our worship to become that event which both speaks to our ambiguity with frankness and compassion and also rises clearly above it to proclaim a righteousness and kingdom not of our own making!

No easy business, worship! One does not simply say "let it all happen." In a delightful treatment of the church's quixotic history of tensions between fantasy and its opposite and the festive and its opposite, Harvey Cox points to the tensions and to those historic moments when the church literally "made fun" of them.[3] There had to be times when such tensions would explode and when we might concoct a "feast of fools" in which the high and mighty could be put down and the lowly elevated, in which the value systems of grace (the last shall be first) and of humanity (rewarding itself with honors) would be turned topsy-turvy and holes punctured in our pomposity and power. Interestingly, the tensions and the reversals focused in the central event of the grace-given and received drama—worship!

Worship is thus, in the words of Robert Hudnut, boldly irrelevant and irreverent. Irrelevant in that, by the world's standards at least, there is no feeding of the hungry, clothing the poor, or any other social assist which the moneyed, still powerful ecclesiastical organization *might* do instead of buying expensive stained glass, rank upon rank of organ, and cushioned seating. You've heard all the criticisms before, and raised a few of your own, most likely. But let us not mix our arguments concerning relevancy. There is indeed a *time,* a *place,* an *event* which is unashamedly *irrelevant.* Instead of giving away food to the undernourished, we come to a banquet to be fed. The Eucharist is caught up into the poetic context and description of worship as an unashamed internalizing of grace by hungry people, a time for both the understanding of, and participating in the mystery of living by more than bread alone.

We also encounter worship as that which is irreverent. There are innumerable historic people, places, and times when the worship of God turned to sheer dance, whether in the frenetic and embarrassing releases of the Feast of Fools in medieval Europe or the ancient dance of David around the ark—much to the disgust of his wife and the delight of the Lord (2 Sam: 6:12–23).

3. Harvey Cox, *Feast of Fools* (Cambridge: Harvard University Press, 1967), pp. 3–6.

ON RECEIVING GIFTS

To chew on the dialectic as it centers its give/receive tensions in worship is also to ponder how most of us have been taught to receive gifts. We have feelings about that. "Is it alright for me to receive the gift?" The implications of that specific emotion are seldom dealt with by the contemporary worshiping community.

Most of us have learned how to internalize the feelings about ourselves which lead us to say, "No, it's *not* alright for me to receive. It's all right for me to *give*! That's my task in life, as a Christian, as one who is given a mission— my task is to give it away!" We leave the tension which the dialectic also applies to our self-understanding through the gospel and settle for significantly less, thus robbing ourselves of a crucial dimension of the worship dynamic: being receivers!

It is as if we insist upon saying to God, "Don't love *me*. I'm not worthy. Just give me a kind of arm's length love, a package I can deliver up to another person in your name." Does this attitude then "buy us" the necessary acceptance which will allow us the freedom to be open receivers? Hardly; it only persists in holding us in check, for never are we able to persuade our conditioned unconscious that we have finally performed enough to allow us now to "accept our *own* acceptance!"[4]

If we permit others to love us, if we allow for any kind of dynamic of love to be given/received, whether in marriage or in church, we leave ourselves somewhat at the mercy of the initiator of that love. Andrew Greeley once pointed out how this dynamic becomes risky business if we permit another to love us and thus to make a claim upon us.[5] Of course we often resist such a process, whether in marriage or in church.

4. See Paul Tillich's sermon, "You Are Accepted," in *Shaking the Foundations* (New York: Scribner, 1950).
5. See Andrew Greeley, "The Fear of Being Loved," *National Catholic Reporter* (January 8, 1969).

If we are loved we "belong" to the one who loves us. The history of that tender relationship has taught us that marital love cannot *possess,* and that God in his love does not presume to *possess,* to own, except once again in the most poetic sense.

We know by our experiences that when we wish to be alone those who love us may *not,* because of the nature of their love for us, leave us alone. We know by our experiences that when we wish to wallow a bit in inexplicable masochism or mediocrity and have our "blue," or down day, those who love us invite us instead to feel whole or great in a way we wish we didn't have to feel at the time; and we think, "How dare you!" We want to be angry and harsh and we are appealed to by love for gentleness and feeling. We want to be moody and we are invited by love to come play and laugh. It's terrible, isn't it?

The very idea of the intimacy of love's relationship, of its terrifying demands, of its insistence upon stripping us of our defenses, all cause unspeakable anguish—in marriages, friendships, and in churches and wherever the dynamic is played out. Yet if we are convinced that we are not the objects of God's love, that we are not his word-to-be-lived-out, that we are not paradoxically his unworthy-yet-"worthed"-by-grace servants and prophets and stewards and lovers, then we will have enormous problems being ourselves in the descriptions and proscriptions to follow.

THE WORSHIPING COMMUNITY

The Community of the Resurrected

The worshiping community, in reenacting the eschatological banquet and celebrating its life in the good news, is first of all the community of the resurrected. Set that, then, within the dialectic. The tension is life/death, life received by giving itself away in a dying daily, as Luther said of the necessity to drown the old Adam in us and live open to the new Adam living in us. It is a living *in* the resurrection which began with our baptism and includes, as expected historic event, our death.[6] Resurrection is, as H. A. Williams contends, the defiance of the absurd, the background of resurrection itself being impossibility. It requires of us an eschatological dimension even while we acknowledge that we live *in* the resurrection just as we await its coming. We are called thus to the urgency of living while living in anticipation: "Watch therefore, for you know neither the day nor the hour" (Matt. 25:13).

> If, as Christians are supposed to believe, Christ *is* the resurrection, it is strange that life for us invariably means business as usual, especially the business we transact with ourselves. Christ's métier is generally considered to be the preservation of the status quo; in individuals a personal psychic status quo and in the church an institutional status quo, provided that in each case there is a respectable measure of reform, in the individual mostly moral and in the church mostly administrative.[7]

This devastating commentary may easily be extended into the place and hour where the drama or lack of it is acted out, made known, and demonstrably believed—the liturgy of word and sacrament—the twin bases for being and acting out who we are in Christ. That the status quo is evident in worship gives us pause to examine this phenomenon from the critical perspective of the resurrection and specifically the worshiping community's reluctance to become the company of the resurrected.

Williams suggests that, because we have made God and worship of him into a cult-idol, the contemporary church views resurrection as an inconvenience to our cult-idol which keeps the lid on literally everything. The advantage of the cult-idol therefore is that it or he cannot do anything significant. This leaves us free to continue on as before or,

---

6. See *The Large Catechism of Martin Luther,* trans. Robert H. Fischer (Philadelphia: Muhlenburg Press, 1959) .

7. H. A. Williams, *True Resurrection* (New York: Harper & Row, 1972) , p. 7.

as I prefer to put it, to control the very expressions of worship themselves, to "make sense" out of our worship, to appeal more to the mind than to the depth of the hungering spirit. So we insulate ourselves against this threat by pushing resurrection into the safe realm of the past or the future. Christ either *was* or he *will be*, our fears keep telling us.

The Community of the Prophetic

As we continue to become receivers in worship, understood as the grace event focused in the eschatological meal, and as we come to understand the radicality and risk of living out our own resurrection, we need also to be held together by the mortar of mission. Chapter 7 will deal with the shape and content of the church in mission. Sufficient for the purpose of giving broader meaning to both meal and hope is the very *idea* of the church as mission. All of the journey inward—its warming touches of acceptance, of therapeutic community, of living out of one's baptism as a resurrected person, of allowing for human vulnerability, and of being generally open to the diversity of the Holy Spirit in and through the lives of others—all of these expressions of the inward journey of grace provide us with the sustenance which will set us on our outward journey of servanthood. That outward journey is always in tension with the inward. The church is both grace-fed and faith-proclaiming, both vertical and horizontal in its relationships, both private and public in its piety, both trusted and trusting, both radically accepted and totally accepting, both loved and loving, both justified and acting toward others in justice.

The church therefore does not have a set of missions, things to do, categories of human needs to fill in Jesus' name, as if we could somehow play with a list of possible ways to justify, even ratify, a faith which must now have some purposes, aims, and goals in concert with others. Business may see its mission in that manner, but not the church.

The church does not have, in the sense of possession or even control, a neat stack of pursuable missions. The church *is* mission, by virtue of its description and by reflection into the depth of the dialectic between the inward and the outward journeys. In worship it is axiomatic that before we can *get,* we must *give,* while at the same time before we can *give,* we must *get.* There is no ordering, no system which neatly packages and enhances our practice of worship. The dialectic, indeed the radical clash, is simply a way of letting us in on a bit of the mystery while parrying our usual blatant attempt to worm our way all the way in and destroy the mystery.

Another way of identifying the clash between the inward element and the prophetic element, the tension involved in "doing the Father's will" even as we are totally absorbed in the *receiving* of that will's love and mercy, is to speak of the confusion of words used over what we *go* to on Sunday mornings. Is it a worship or a service? Is it possible to serve God in worship or do we serve him by serving our brother and sister? God needs nothing, least of all our "proper" words, or even a remembered incantation of our omissions and commissions. But we certainly need that sort of catharsis. So we say on our bulletin board, so as to neatly separate the inseparable: "Enter to worship; leave to serve."

DIMENSIONS OF WORSHIP

Worship as we experience it at CCS includes a number of dimensions or goals:

1. Genuinely participatory; involving laity and clergy, men and women, adults and children.
2. Sensitive in the language, symbols, and actions it uses in the liturgical drama.
3. Centering itself in the mystery of the hope-filled Eucharist, willing to risk and share its faith and unfaith in openness, expecting and seeking forgiveness and reconciliation.
4. Maintaining a perception about who we are in the face of God, thus keeping our sense of humor and joy in the fact that "He still likes us" after all.

5. Allowing for the liturgy to be thematically diverse so as to teach, but also to allow the liturgical (historical) drama to become participatory action as against mere verbiage.

These dimensions by no means "detail" all there is to say about worship. They suggest much about attitudes, setting, common understanding and expectations, and certainly about the "ownership" of the materials and symbols of worship by the *whole* community of faith. I begin there.

1) At CCS we try to encourage ownership of worship, even in its thematic planning stages and right on down to the selection of hymns. Participation is in depth as well as in breadth.

On a volunteer basis, and with plenty of encouragement and help from the pastor, musicians, and liturgical deacons, we ask people to become "host family" for a particular Sunday. This means forming a "family" for the day for those who are single or who want to work with particular people in the development of a liturgical, biblical, theological, or social theme in which they have special interest, and for others it means gathering the nuclear family together for a heightened sense of participation in worship.

The idea behind the "host family" is, at first glance, elementary: to invite meaningful involvement on the part of the laity in worship. Of course, churches can involve laypeople by having all sorts of tasks set before them. For at least a generation or more the church has been very effective at this kind of involvement of the laity through the assignment of tasks, some of which have been accidentally demeaning and many of which offer no significant sense of *ownership*. At CCS, designation of a host family is not simply a way to have people other than the minister read certain scriptures in order to demonstrate that "the laypeople in this church are involved!" We have something else in mind, especially that the various actions of the liturgy or the drama itself may become beneficial for the growth of the persons involved.

First, the host family is asked to bring intercessions on behalf of the community of the faithful. This means that a prayer which invokes the grace of God on behalf of various people and conditions must become a fresh issue for the family during the prior week. Even the by-product of the family's perceptions in coming together to talk about their own concerns for people, for those hospitalized or hurting in marriages or divorces, for institutions, governments, groups, is nearly enough to make the *process* as worthwhile as the results. There is a wholesome dynamic whenever a family can sit down together and ask each other to come to terms, through the form of intercessory prayer, with people and events they hold as significant. For whom should the grace of God be invoked? What news has this world of ours made this past week which causes us to enter into the depth of prayerful concern? Who in our own midst has a particular need which not only requires God's gracefull attention but ours too? The whole emotional undergirding of intercession is a particularly meaningful way not only to name names and state conditions of concern before God but also to announce before other human beings that this is the way you as a family read the signs of your own day and come to terms with them as expressions of your own faith.

Some of us who have lived in families in this mid-twentieth century have seen how easy it is for each of us to go our own way and for frustration to fester inside. We somehow never find enough time to get it expressed in the full view of the ones we claim to love and who love us. It is hoped that when people become a host family the very necessity of having to deal with the themes which the scriptures-for-the-day indicate, along with the concerns with which one attempts to come to grips in the intercessions, will all together provide enough of a hint that such family times can be anguishingly beautiful. But the anguish of meaningful communication even within our own homes has to start someplace. Why not within the context of the word of God as good news, and as we come to grips with the evidence of the news we ourselves make throughout the week?

We encourage the members of the family to take turns reading the Old Testament, the Epistle, and the Gospel. To read loud and clear is essential, of course. This simple concern possibly is overlooked, but most of us become a bit nervous when we find a few hundred people listening to what we say. We soon learn that such readings are not for "show," even though an appropriate sense of the dramatic may often be applied, for example, in taking gospel discourses and letting the ancient personages come alive through having their parts read by various family members, including children. Many times the actual historical event shines through brilliantly when it is "acted out" with devotion and care. No one ever intended biblical readings to be flat and without the enthusiasm of a genuine human empathy. Creativity is certainly in order in the telling of the truth of God. Let the family decide together.

At the time of the offering, the family of the day is given the special privilege of being hosts in a very real sense by bringing the gifts of bread and wine for all to share in the Eucharist. What symbolizes best, for that particular family, the elements used by Jesus "on the night when he was betrayed?" Usually common bread is used and a red wine symbolizing blood. Beyond the obvious, however, there is the preference of the family. Some families have baked bread; others have used rye, or white, and still others matzo or unleavened bread. Some families have understood the wine in terms of what they would serve at a very special party in their own home, while others see the wine as a vin du jour or common table wine such as Jesus might have used. There is freedom to set the symbolic tone as well as to express verbally anything concerning the family decisions, feelings, and questions for that day.

Children are encouraged to assist by passing and receiving the offering plates and bringing them to the altar. They also light the altar candles and assist at the offertory procession.

The whole family may wish to help pass out bulletins, hymnals, or notices at the beginning of the worship. Contemporary readings are also encouraged and suggested in order to provide for interpretive, instructive, or illuminating commentary through the writings, authors, or journalists of our day.

2) Language is a matter of special concern. We find ourselves in the midst of revolution concerning language. Christians are beginning to understand that inclusive language, language which does not deliberately or accidentally exclude people, is essential. Liturgical references to the "men of God" or even use of the generic "man" or "mankind" may not evidence the kind of care in portraying the faith that would seek to take seriously the reactions of a growing number of concerned women.

Language, happily, is not the only means of telling each other our story. If liturgy is drama, then that drama includes great varieties of musical expression: jazz, folk, spirituals, and so-called classical music, all of which help to articulate the good news. Dance and creative art join the old visual aids and the newer more satisfying video, film, and multi-media event to keep worship from becoming stultified, pedantic, and blathering.

In the CCS structure, there is an informal "care committee" concerned with language and the arts, a group of sensitive people who remind those of us who are so dependent upon the word that there are other ways of speaking the truth and proclaiming the mystery. Every congregation could use some kind of watchdog group in order that we, who, as individuals, live out of one set of experiences, feelings, pains, and hopes, might become enriched by the variety of gifts in others around us. Diversity within congregational life should be a blessing, not a point of impending judgment and division.

Let language, music, art, and all manner of human expression and communication flourish that we might grow, realize diversity, and become a more inclusive community. Otherwise what does the word "catholic" mean for us?

3) At the Eucharist every Sunday morning at 10 and Thursday evening at 7:30, CCS gathers around the altar to receive the Body and the Blood. Mystery and joy intermingle. The horizontal relationship within the grace-feeding of the Eucharist is deliberately pressed upon us all as we pass the chalice from one to another. As the cup is held, the one who gives the cup says to the recipient, "This is for our reconciliation." Invariably there is a peculiar sensitivity one to another because of the significance of the act itself. One cannot long pass and receive the cup of reconciliation without coming to know the persons who are, by Christ and his mystery, *in communion* with you.

Soon one realizes that faith does not automatically grow upon faith as if somehow unaware of the dialectic. Reconcilation means, in the language of children, to "make up," and making up presupposes a fight or at least a condition of noncommunion or separation. Precisely that kind of restless alienation, that sort of movement toward reconcilation, is what causes faith to grow in honesty through genuine human intercourse. It is our basic alienation, our separateness, our doubts and unbelief which are in vital tension with our faith, our sense of togetherness and wholeness of being. In the Gospel of Mark the believing father who could honestly say "but help my unbelief" was also open to growth in grace and free of illusions about his own faith.

Faith itself cannot exist within a vacuum. Faith is mirrored in its own unfaith. Faith does not grow *on* faith but *by* the doubts which raise up questions and new searchings of the heart and mind.

Luther, in describing the growth of the human spirit in Christ, was careful to spell out a picture of God with an *opus alienum,* a left hand, a hand which performed God's "alien work," punching us, tapping us, and otherwise reminding us of our imperfect state. It is by the left hand that we are driven to the right hand, the *opus proprium*, God's proper work of forgiving love. Both, like doubt and trust, have their appointed duties and significant investment in the destiny of the human. That such give and take should *both* occur within the worship dynamic is crucial.

It is very possible that the minister, through the homily, will have to set the tone of vulnerability, letting the congregation know that "even" the clergy has doubts. I am constantly reminded that clergy for all too many centuries have been invested—accidentally, I trust—with suits of the armor of faith that are made, as it were, without seams.

For the worship leader to welcome the worshipers into his or her humanity is a good thing. In fact, it may be the necessary reminder that here in worship is the one place, the one occasion of the many in which we gather as human beings, which calls for the utmost candor and honesty concerning who we are. How foolish to pretend to appear before God and/or each other as *simply* the people of faith. We are also the people of unfaith and of important doubt, of pain and of remembered guilt, both real and neurotic— often we are unable to tell one from the other. The very symbolism of our customary dressing up, of a caricatured seriousness, of being "proper," and of using "Sunday manners" all divulge the fact that few of us have allowed the important tensions between honest faith and honest doubt to escape into the heavy air of corporate Sunday hypocrisy.

Relax. God knows what you know! At least.

4) The idea of injecting a sense of humor into corporate worship is also crucial because humor is a "serious" component in our humanity. We are at least *homo ludens*.[8] Humor is appropriate to worship as surely as the tension between the holy and the human. That we approach the holy with pomposity and the occasional need to "make a

---

8. Johan Huizinga, *Homo Ludens* (Boston: Beacon Press, 1950). *Homo ludens* refers to man at play.

deal" is genuinely funny. That there are often tears mixed into our laughter indicates that we know the laugh is on us and that God laughs with us as the one who created our humor potential and who knows of the possible foibles inherent in our human condition.

Many theologians of our time are intentionally bringing the element of humor into their understanding of the life of Christ and of the nature of the church, through their biblical insights in particular. Nelvin Vos, in a disarmingly pithy little book,[9] quotes Christopher Fry, saying:

> Do we waste the evening
> Commiserating with each other about
> The unhygienic condition of our worm-cases?
> For God's sake, shall we laugh.[10]

More important, Vos helps us understand the "three faces of laughter," namely, the clown, in which he has us all vicariously identify with Jesus as harlequin; and the contrasting faces of the wit and the butt. Both wit and butt have been found in literature, and often in each other: whenever we become amused by someone else's embarrassment in falling on the banana peel (the wit then stands above it all and laughs) or when we fall on the peel and quickly look around to see if anyone has noticed (the butt simply receives the ludicrous and absurd). In the clown, there is the ability to accept the ludicrous. When the clown falls, he is amused by his own ludicrousness. He is neither victim nor victor but in a sense both. He is the victor because he has accepted the role of victim.[11]

Laughter is a way we have of being appropriately self-critical, a way of being able to both see and appreciate our own pretentiousness, and there is no greater temptation to become pretentious than when we sound the call to wor-

---

9. Nelvin Vos, *For God's Sake Laugh* (Richmond: John Knox Press, 1967).

10. Christopher Fry, *The Lady's Not for Burning* (New York: Oxford University Press, 1950), p. 49. Used by permission.

11. Vos, *For God's Sake Laugh*, pp. 38–39.

ship. Preachers (at the word "preacher" there are many who giggle nervously) "mount" the pulpit like some kingly throne to "foghorn behind the Imperial bird."

There is no way, with the perspective of honest humor available, to keep our "cool" in church as poised devotees of the Infinite. We laugh at our finiteness and so increase both the distance and the closeness of the Infinite within our worship.

5) Finally, worship has the occasional, even usual task of teaching, of informing. Liturgy as such can be a didactic tool. If so, then why stay with one set of words as if, by their repetition, even memorization, we cause worship to become less of a struggle to *think,* more of a familiar or remembered *feel* and, therefore, more authentic. Rubbish! Let there be as much diversity in the liturgy of the word as there are words by which we may proclaim God's truth.

Let there be catholicity in form and diversity in expression. The maintenance of a format—a flow for worship which regularly includes confession and absolution, the reading and interpreting of scripture in orderly thematic fashion, the prayer elements of intercession, petition, thanksgiving, the canon of the Eucharist, all in historic place—is sufficient to welcome people into a truly apostolic and catholic setting. Here, with the saints of all ages, we *do,* we enact, we engage in the drama, step by step, event by event.

But there is no reason for biblical themes and Christian teachings to be reserved only for select days. At CCS we find ourselves moving through the church year with a variety of liturgical themes, set within the centuries-old tradition of receiving word and sacrament, yet with the urgent expectation of a people born anew this day in a new resurrection. Our experiments have been many:

Advent—a liturgy of creating anew (for beginning a new church year and covenanting together)
—a wake up liturgy (the theme of the prophetic call for Advent)

Christmas—a candlelight eucharist (including themes on
              Incarnation occurring in places, people, and
              events)

Epiphany—Twelfth Night (with lovely traditions from
              Austria: the burning of greens, the last of
              the carols to be sung, the children finding
              the hidden peas in the eucharistic loaf not
              used in the Communion)

Lent—a liturgy on human authenticity (identifying with
           the vulnerability of the passion cast)

Easter—the traditional Midnight Vigil (with baptism and
           Celebration of Life)

Pentecost—a liturgy on the Breath of God

Occasional—a celebration of the temporary
          —a celebration of work and leisure (for Labor
            Day Sunday)
          —a liturgy of discovery or "search for roots"
            (for Reformation)

The worship life of the church is significant, and a kind
of barometer for all other dimensions of the life of the congregation. Is it a freeing, empathetic, people-touching time?
Can I laugh and cry and come out from behind the protec-
tive shields I feel forced to wear all week? Can I sense the
continuing movement and thrust of the worship? Is it a
drama which includes me and my life and hopes? Can I *do*
the liturgy, act it out with others? Do I see faces or merely
backs? May I handle the holy? May I question the holy?
May I appreciate the holy—and be handled, questioned, and
confronted by the holy? May I be *me* at worship?

So, Eucharist, hope, vulnerability, mystery, doubt, resurrection, humor, sensitivity, participation—these are the
themes of our common journey inward, the very gifts which
send us out into the journey of servanthood. Though we
can never simply *remain* at the place where the inward
journey takes us in worship, it nevertheless is the place
where we may truly be held together!

5. Wrestling with the Angel: Becoming the Church Through the Yearly Covenant

That same night he rose . . . crossed the ford of the Jabbok. . . . And Jacob was left alone. And there was one that wrestled with him until daybreak. . . . "Let me go, for day is breaking." But Jacob answered, "I will not let you go unless you bless me." He said, "Your name shall no longer be Jacob, but Israel, because you have been strong against God, you shall prevail against men."

—Genesis 32:22,24,28 (JB)

If in union with Christ we have imitated his death, we shall also imitate him in his resurrection. We must realize that our former selves have been crucified with him to destroy this sinful body and to free us from the slavery of sin.   —Romans 6:5,6 (JB)

The old man therefore follows unchecked the inclinations of his nature if he is not restrained and suppressed by the power of Baptism. On the other hand, when we become Christians, the old man daily decreases until he is finally destroyed. That is what it means to plunge into Baptism and daily come forth again.   —The Large Catechism of Martin Luther, *The Book of Concord*

BELONGING AND BEING COUNTED

The Apostle Paul chastised the young Christian congregation at Corinth when word got to him that there were some who claimed to "belong to Cephas," some to Apollo, some to Paul. Many of us empathize with such feelings and loyalties which have been expressed to various pastoral and lay leaders who have made deep impressions within our congregational experience. But Paul rightly objected to the idea of "belonging." "Has Christ been parcelled out?", Paul asked them (1 Cor. 1:13, JB).

What does it mean for us to "belong" to a church? The ecclesiastical categories of belonging are many, including for example: "baptized member," "confirmed member," "communing member," "member in good standing" (usually communing and/or making a gift of record at least once a year), and "lapsed member." The list could go on as far as the imagination envisions the various ways in which humans act out their voluntary relationships toward the church as structure.

But the listing of categories, usable or not, does not answer the vexing question of belonging, a continuously festering question in a society which has developed volunteerism to such a finely honed human art. In recent years there has not been the certainty or the clarity of meaning that once attached to belonging to family, nation, neighborhood, denomination, or local church. In my ministry, I have seen old and traditional loyalties fade or become frustrated through mobility and other factors, especially among the young.

Today, however, people of all ages seem eager once again to rediscover the roots of their belonging. At CCS when Reformation Sunday comes around, we find ourselves listening to a different introit, one that helps us authenticate our continuing search for roots:

> The person who merely goes on living and never asks what is the meaning of this life is like the person who tells pointless stories. Renewal, both personal and congregational, comes about through the anguishing call to sort out the real from the illusive, the ultimate from the transitory, the true from the fickle, and the priceless treasure from the earthenware vessel in which it is set. To be truly Christian,

truly human, we must not allow the questions of our roots
to cease stirring within us.[1]

The liturgy then offers up some familiar word-pictures pertaining to our sense of belonging in a "litany of discovering
roots":

Leader: We remember the earthiness of places,
     events and things and how they give
     us a sense of lasting roots;

R/ of memories of a house on a certain street,
   childhood surroundings,
   a place to "go back to,"
   a picture of home.

Leader: We recall the touch of human commitment
     through people who are close to us,
     and of roots called family;

R/ of surnames and histories which are ours alone,
   shared memories with brothers and sisters,
   parental love too awe-ful for words,
   commitment to another in word and deed.

Leader: We recognize the enticement in the untried
     and unknown and how it lures us into the
     secret excitement of finding uncharted roots;

R/ of delicious phantasies,
   gratification in a new thing done well,
   and exchange of deep secrets,
   the surprising gifts from love willingly
    received.

Leader: We recoil at the times of our stout defense
     through mere words which served as fences
     to hem us in and cause our roots to be
     stunted;

R/ of memorized confessions not yet ours,
   dogmas angrily defended,

---

1. From "Reformation: A Liturgy of Discovering—A Search for Roots" (1975).
Privately printed by and available from CCS Publishing House, Downers
Grove, Illinois.

"blessed assurances" not yet fought for,
hopes and joys not yet risked.

Leader: We respond to the simple and profound love
which is yours for us, O God, undeserved
and unconditional,
and the resurrection roots planted for us by
your Son in our own soil;

R/   of the freedom to live before we die,
accepting our own acceptance,
our unashamed struggle to believe and not
believe,
of mystery in being reconciled in the
sacrament.

Leader: We recover our roots in you so slowly and
tenuously, O Lord, and in the human
community around us.
Help us, by your grace, to sense the integrity
and purposes of your will, that we may live
justly and with peace;

R/.   to touch and be touched,
to risk and respond without fear,
to fail and receive support,
to use humor as well as pain in the gentle
discoveries of being your children.

Leader: Hear us, O God.

R/   Amen.[2]

A NEW CONCERN FOR IDENTITY

The concerns of belonging—particularly in a serious religious setting—have never been more evident than in the latter twentieth century. Are we simply to be counted, categorized, and given a denominational identity? For some thinking and feeling people, that process, complete with its "traveling form," the ubiquitous "letter of transfer," is not adequate. To be limited to the keeping of records is also

2. Ibid.

not enough for the feeling parish or denomination. Robert C. Dodds, in an article for the *Christian Century,* proposed general church membership based upon the very argument Paul used with the divisive little congregation in Corinth; namely, the uniqueness of our baptism. Our identity is therefore in that we are all baptized in Christ.[3] Because so many of us seem to require more specific identity and because some people desire to or are caught up in maintaining lifelong fidelity to particular traditions, such a proposal will probably not be widely accepted. Oddly, however, most of us practice the thesis that says, "anyone who belongs to one (Christian tradition) belongs also to ours."

The preservation of our local identities and integrities is of greater importance to more and more people. The very possibility of regional or area churches or denominations coming into being, at the expense of the more expansive national bodies, is evidence that such a direction is being taken quite seriously by some ecclesiastical leadership.

Of great importance also is that point of Christian identity beyond our common baptism which seems to be lost or shrouded in our day, our peculiar behavioral *style*: "They'll know we are Christians by our love." There may also be some undeniable romance in such yearnings for identity, since a clearly visible style of radical love in Christ does not automatically insure a prior commitment nor perception of the radical nature or direction of his teachings.

A particular life-style with its concomitant religious practices has, throughout the centuries, been a distinguishing feature of orthodox Jews. Observers have been made sensitive to the ways in which they are "different." Dietary regulations, prayer shawls, fixing the doorways for holy days, sabbath rules, situational behavior patterns—all help the Jew to be set apart from all others. The question, for Christians, is: Are we also to be set apart in similar manner? Are style, difference from others, distinctiveness of religious regu-

3. Robert C. Dodds, "The Meaning of Membership," *Christian Century* (September, 1968).

lations to be the distinguishing marks of our "membership" in the church of Jesus Christ? I think not. Attractive as these clearly discernible styles are, they are not of the essence for the Christian.

THE CHRISTIAN STYLE

As already discussed in chapter 2, the church has understood and occasionally practiced a critical self-understanding predicated on the "role" of the new Adam, the Christ *incognito* amid all peoples and conditions, the people peculiarly sensitive to the tensions between the clearly identified religious insider and the assumed nonreligious outsider. Because this "style" is not to be casually overlooked in the midst of a discussion concerning belonging and the meaning of church membership, we are called to search for identities and forms which transcend those which, however attractive initially, may be ostentatious and possibly coercive.

The question then might be: How do we keep growing? How do we know and feel our true identity in Christ? How do we allow for the Spirit to push us beyond the traditional practice of an exclusive congregational membership maintained as a roll of individual names on a parish record? How can "belonging" mean more than a specified affiliation with a structure?

There are a number of models to help us answer those crucial and highly charged questions.

A Distinctive Biblical Model

Ever since 1970, CCS has come to grips with a biblical model used once a year as a means or tool for self-evaluation and reassessment of "belonging" within the voluntary association called church. The model is from Genesis 32 and pictures Jacob in an all night wrestling match with the angel. The Hebrew word-picture is most delightful in this imaginative chapter. Jacob clearly is at odds with his brother, at loggerheads with his own destiny, and, one presumes, in need of rediscovering his roots in his own Abrahamic traditions and in the sense in which he personally belonged to his father's and grandfather's Yahweh!

He wrestled in order to shape and sharpen his questions to discover and to quicken his inner being to the whole complexity of feelings which some today would identify as ontological shocks. Who am I? Where do I fit? What are my questions? Where are my footings? Who is my God *now*?

Jacob risked making Yahweh his own Lord rather than merely a spiritual property inherited from his ancestors. Such an effort, while risky, can also be healthy for us.

Jacob's long night proved his humanhood. He was, after all, held together by more than reason and will; there also was emotion within him, and the ability to dream and to hope. He hoped therefore for himself, for his life and his future, and he knew he had to reckon with, even struggle against, the God of his very creation and being. Clearly Jacob was a man, not a turnip. He was dynamic, in tension, not simply planted, awaiting a higher being's whim to someday pluck him up.

Jacob belonged: to God and to himself—and to the interworking between the two. Covered beneath the blanket of his finiteness, he was constantly being called to kick the covers off. The very nature of the complex relationship between the human creature and the divine Maker implies struggle.

As the new day awoke for Jacob he discovered himself pinning the angel down, making him say "uncle," quite in the same manner as an "early" Luther damned the very presence of a demanding God. Nearly everyone for whom faith has had concrete meaning and articulation has gone through such a struggle. Call it the struggle to genuinely belong.

Jacob is a healthy model not only because of his struggle but also for other reasons held up in the vivid and exciting story of his encounter with the angel. He determined that he had been in the Presence of the Holy One and so named the place of his faith-anguish Peniel, meaning "I have seen God face to face"; his encounter was therefore in the setting of a worship experience.

More important, however, was the angel's statement at the end of the struggle: "Your name shall no longer be Jacob, but Israel, because you have been strong against God" (Gen. 32:28, JB). That is, Jacob had prevailed, had become more definably a human with a destiny and belonging vested in Yahweh. Jacob felt this power, which, interestingly, he himself had initiated out of the wellsprings of his own questions and doubts. His story reminds us of the continual attempts by Old and New Testament personalities and poets to force God's hand, as it were, to request, from their own plight or need for clearer vision, that God himself "rend the heavens" and come down. Jacob's theophany was a way in which God may "come down." For Jacob, it changed his name, gave him a new destiny and future, and thus a sense of belonging.

The Jacob model can be coupled with Paul's model of dying in the baptismal waters, or with Luther's pithy interpretation of the necessity for the "old man" in us to die daily, to give way to the new man in Christ and therefore in us. With these models and others we at CCS make every attempt to invest the meaning of membership with that of the continual struggle toward a sensitized belonging.

A Liturgical Model

On the last Sunday in the church year and just one week before Advent, the CCS membership, or rather those who have covenanted together for the year just gone by, are released from that membership covenant. The introit sets the tone, fleshes out the meaning of dissolution of a one-year covenant together, and provides us with the invitation for the new struggle:

> We gather for an auspicious occasion. Today is a day of conclusions, of endings. On this final Sunday of the church year, we symbolize the completion of the covenants we have

made with each other and in Christ during the year. We know God's unconditional love and grace for us—his covenant with us is everlasting. But we also know our need to renew, to rethink, to have rebirth of the content of our covenanting together, and of our mission as his church on earth. We are therefore reminded of Jesus saying, "Anyone who would keep his life must lose it." In this death-to-birth process we come now to unload all our misspent failures of the past and the terrors of haunting guilt of days long gone. Christ bears our burdens of past sins. Let us begin to covenant afresh with him through each other, with purposes for the year ahead akin to his love for us.[4]

It is at this point that we take a symbolic week-between-covenants (from the last Sunday in the church year to the first Sunday in Advent) to wrestle with the shape and scope of our new commitment. Then, during any of the Advent Sundays, we come to sign our names to a simple parchment which reads, "The Covenant of the Community of Christ the Servant for 1978." Everyone is also provided with opportunity and time to speak to the whole community concerning their own intended ministry, hopes, requests, and plans. It is also a time for special attention to be given to those making their initial covenant with CCS. We especially want to know them as people, to learn their intentions toward engaging in corporate worship and ministry with us, and to hear of their dreams and needs within the therapeutic community. Also, those new to the community may sign the covenant at any time during the year with the understanding that the covenant—the content and shape of our mutual commitments to ministry—concludes on the final Sunday in the church year.

The Shape of Our Struggle

Within the format of both worship and homily, we speak of the fundamental dimensions of our struggle. They are many. They are essentially of the gospel:

4. From "A Liturgy of Dissolution and Creating Anew" (1973). Privately printed by and available from CCS Publishing House, Downers Grove, Illinois.

—We cannot begin the struggle *on cue,* just because we have come to a designated time in the liturgical calendar. We are free to say "not now."

—We are already God's by baptism. Our initial and real "struggle" was already fought for us in Christ's death for us, and in our participation in that Good Friday event and the victory of Easter through our baptism.

—We take time to covenant (recovenant) because we have already received an unconditional promise or covenant from God. Our covenant thus takes on the character of a simple response to an ever-present and unfickle grace.

—We acknowledge being part of the church catholic, sharing in mission, and needing to rethink our tenets and sighting the fresh scope which this new day brings to the membership which we affirm.

—We need whatever psychological or symbolic sense there might be in declaring, before God and each other, this year's covenant completed and ended. We need to take time and space to offer up our sins of omission and commission and to be freed from the occasional tyrannies of the past.

—We sense our need for new beginnings, new hopes to be shared aloud, new possibilities and needs to be said and heard by each other.

—We do not wish to play games with assumptions concerning membership on a local level nor with all the categories such as "lapsed" or "in good standing." We wish rather to face the risk of literally having to go "out of business" as a congregation if we are merely becoming perfunctory as servants of Christ's word and will. Besides, whoever gave the clergy or the institutional church the right to *control* Christian identity and the meaning of "being Christian" for anyone?

COVENANTING

The Institutional Covenant

During our conversations together at this time of covenanting we at CCS gratefully acknowledge that there are many ministries which we as individuals cannot accomplish without designated structures. The individual needs the power of the group and its extensive power, ministry, and priorities which the national and international bodies are able to provide. We seek fresh appreciation of certain structures that prevail year after year because they minister to us, speaking to our continuing condition and need, or because they provide sustenance to others in ways that none of us could do individually.

In covenanting we mention these ministries pertinent to structural or institutional covenants, ministries that go beyond ·the usual ecclesial structuring, because at this risky, question-laden stand called experimental, where we have been doing business for a few years now, we believe we should articulate these areas as specifically as we are able:

1. We covenant with each other in the Christian value-setting processes, especially education of the young. Because we are all "in formation" in pursuit of our becoming, set within the tensions of the human dialectic, we need and wish for structures of education which will serve and meet those ends, and not simply information sessions. But particularly because we are to be responsible as adult parents for our dependent and impressionable children, we accept our roles of primary value-setters for them, not wishing to abdicate that responsibility to any "amateur" adult. We therefore are content to seek structures within the church as teaching instruments which will help us as adults and parents, and thus we believe strongly in adult Christian education as a continuing and challenging part of the congregation's self-structuring process. Further, we appreciate any and all supportive roles the church may play in the value-setting of the young as long as it does not consciously usurp basic parental rights and privileges.

2. We covenant with each other to form any and all necessary structures which will serve Christ's purposes, such as community organizations for social justice and change,

and liturgical deacons' training for purposes of becoming sensitive to the historic dynamics of worship. At the same time, we understand the foolishness of bringing into being new structures which may become self-perpetuating after they outlive their intended usefulness. Therefore, we also assume that structures will relate to viable and well-defined ministries and that such ministries will be part of the genuine life of the people and not simply inventions of the denomination or clergy. Further, each ministry might give serious consideration to a termination date, or at least to periodic review by both insiders and outsiders as to its strengths and weaknesses.[5]

The Individual Covenant

There is also an articulation each year of what it means to be an individual within the corporate body of Christ. Here we encourage the individual to "infiltrate" (see chapter 7) as a Christ incognito into the *already working* power structures of our society.

Our purpose is not to build intramural structures which are essentially powerless and cared for only by those who feel responsible for the maintenance of those groupings. Instead we join the ACLU, a community organization, a town council, a regional planning board, or any number of power-oriented and change-producing organizations. To act in and through existing and functioning groups is to place your voice and your will, and to whatever extent they reside

5. The serving ministries embraced within the CCS corporate covenant in one recent year included: ACLU office help, CCS Publishing Board of Volunteers in Publishing (V.I.P.), Du Page Mental Health Volunteers, Liturgical Deacons, Jazz Vespers ministry, Teaching Parish Liaison Committee, teen ministry, United Citizens Organization, Hunger Committee, Christmas School Program, CCS Campers group, Education Counsel, Health Club, Singles' Workshop, Annual Pastors' Workshop in Parish Renewal, Marriage Seminar Committee, Chilean Refugee Committee, Health Fair, Proposal to Lilly Foundation: Network for the Exchange of Ministries and Outreach, Ministry in Film and Media (Family Film Night), Library Committee, Children's Program support staff, confirmation adjunct teachers, music program, Maintenance Committee, Synodical representatives, relation with renters and space users, political action groups (short-term and specific), Plunge "mother" and arrangements group, and church council.

in Christ, your Christian witness, into the context where life is actually being lived out in today's world.

To Covenant or Not to Covenant

What of those whose struggles seem to indicate a reluctance to any kind of affiliation within a covenanting Christian structure? What kind of psychological preparation do today's clergy have to handle the situation of someone actually confronting him or her and discussing the probability of dropping out of the life of the church? Usually there can be polite and pious wringing of the hands over parish dropouts, and words like "they don't understand or care," can be spoken easily within the counsel of the committed because the "they" being talked about *are also usually absent.* The lapsed are usually disinterested or dissuaded folk and therefore not likely to be invited into questioning or struggling, but left to private criticizing or simply doubting. It is too bad that such anguish is not a real part of the life—the acknowledged risk—of the church itself.

The decision *not* to covenant has occurred at CCS a few times. For some, CCS has been their "last try" at the church and we have not met their expectations nor hopes. For others, CCS has been too radical, too intentional, or "too heavy" despite the celebratory atmosphere, or sometimes because of it.

In a few instances there have been those whose wrestling has indicated their felt need for "a year off" from formal affiliations. During that time, we try to remain in touch while affirming their right to say "no" to the organizational church. For some adults, this is the first time in their lives that they have been given permission to rebel against church or God. There is often a good deal of tragic sublimation of such anger against church and God, often only to please parents or society. There is pain here because in most instances there has also been a good measure of human investment, in being therapeutic with each other, and now all of that seems to be in jeopardy.

But there is also another factor to deal with. I put it in a series of what Normal Habel would call interrobangs[6]—of statements within the question itself. First, how closely identified with *our* local parish must the Kingdom of God become? Is *ours* the only set of experiences one needs or are there differing needs which might be met through a diversity of Christian experiences? If the Kingdom is broader and richer than any local parish, what does that say about relationships with neighboring congregations of various persuasions? Have we mutual needs? Finally, is it not possible truly to accept people at the point where they may actually be in their faith-unfaith tensions and struggles?

Even parish ministries and "non-Christian" voluntary organizations may become supportive and necessary associations for people at various stages of their struggle. The jazz musicians who express their life-values on Sunday afternoons within Jazz Vespers at CCS do not all do so because they are professing Christians or hold membership in some congregation. Few do. Many come because they are friends of Burrell Gluskin, our resident jazz composer, and friends of mine as we have come to know and understand each other. Many come because they trust me when I say, "Help us understand who your God is through your music," or "No strings attached, play what is inside you. That is your integrity. We appreciate it and accept it."

A jazz drummer was setting up behind the altar one day on the makeshift band stand. He had not met me and saw my clerical collar as I came to greet him. His first words spoke volumes for so many who walk the tightrope between the Kingdom of God and local congregations: "Hey man, nothing personal, but I don't even believe in Druids." As it turned out, he has become a good friend. My guess is

6. Norman Habel, *Interrobang* (Philadelphia: Fortress Press, 1969).

that he believes in much more than he dares to risk saying, especially within the setting of the church where he has admitted feeling uncomfortable and often "used." We don't especially talk "church" or "Christ" or "covenant," but still we have learned to trust and love each other. He knows that CCS is radically Christian. He sees the balloons up for various seasons of the church year and knows they represent resurrection. He hears and sees commitment all around him. He comes, however, because he is a vital part of our mutual covenanting.

We do not judge his nonbelief. We encourage his belief, for surely he has such even though it is spoken, played, or felt in ways to which the church may be largely unaccustomed. Who then is outsider here and who is insider?

So within the deliberately covenanting community in Jesus Christ, there may be people passing through a variety of stages and struggles, even a variety of parish organizations, without affirming a loyalty to Christ, the Christian tradition, or the existence and purposes of the parish. But the covenanting community understands and lives nurturingly with —indeed is itself numbered among—those who wrestle with the angel.

6. Teaching Adults and Playing with Children: The Educational Task

The third great invention at the end of the eighteenth and beginning of the nineteenth century was the Sunday school. Originally designed to bridge sacred and secular worlds, it came more and more to serve the religious world in a private way. . . . Religious education in the home never was able to compete with it, and the rise of Sunday schools seemed to many parents to relieve them of the responsibility for religious education.

—Martin E. Marty, *Righteous Empire*

The Small Catechism . . . In the plain form in which they are to be taught by the head of the family . . .
—*Luther's Catechism*

The religious formation of the child, including conscience formation, is the responsibility of the parents. It always has been and always will be.

—O'Neil and Donovan,
Children, Church, and God

Let the children come to me, and do not hinder them; for to such belongs the kingdom of God.
—Luke 18:16

ASSUMPTIONS AND PROBLEMS

For well over a hundred years churches have assumed that children constitute the focal point of formal Christian education. Further, we have assumed that the appropriate structure for that formal education is the Sunday school. Though Robert Raikes founded the Sunday school in 1780 to keep "ragamuffins" off the streets and to help close the gap between those in the general society who were illiterate and those who wished to give credibility to the church as an educational institution, we have turned it into an institution in and of itself for purposes of Christian teaching.

Our assumptions were innocent enough. Here is a self-serving educational arm of the denominational point of view. Here is a credible method of practicing our beliefs, albeit among ourselves, with impressionable youngsters. Here is a vital parental assist in planting precious and tenuous seeds in young lives in order that they may not stray from the "truth" in later years. Here is a working model of a greatly expanded catechizing process which our fast-paced world sorely needs. And finally, as a by-product, here is an opportunity for adults—usually lay volunteers—to give themselves, their talents, and most important, their love of children. Our motives have indeed been impressive.

But the assumptions are now being called into question. Why? Is it merely because we have so often placed such total dependence upon the Sunday school, even making it into a cultural idol—our primary teaching vehicle—and thus often trivializing the importance of the more basic unit of values-imitation and life-orientation; namely, the family? That might be reason enough to call any structure we begin to worship and depend upon into question. But there are other factors as well.

Though it may seem as if we are light-years removed from the ages of the Enlightenment and the Industrial Revolution, we must admit that it is only since then—within a relatively recent time frame—that we began to see the family decline on the educational scene. The change proceeded rapidly as our desires multiplied for better formal education and more abundant specialized education with a view to enabling students to become "a success" in a world dedicated to heightened consumption, competitiveness in the market-place, and a quest for the leisure life.

As a result of these developments the Sunday school too enjoyed an unprecedented period of growth. The young crowd into classrooms of all types preparing themselves for life, we figured—why not also in the church? The Sunday school became a parenting-substitute vehicle for the passing on of religious values from generation to generation. We invested it heavily with our traditions, hopes, and dreams concerning life, death, morality, and ethics—those vital matters which otherwise might have been zealously reserved for the increasingly fragile and beleaguered family. All of this weakened the family as a teaching unit, a unit which had formerly had good feelings about its ability to pass on values and patterns and traditions. The family became educationally unsure of itself.

But a tragic divorce, or at least momentary separation, is taking place in our day between child and parent (s). As a result we are only now beginning to question the wisdom of our dependency upon parent-substitute structures. By depending upon the Sunday school—or better yet, *pretending* it was all we needed—we have given over and trivialized the most visceral of learning processes, that which not only occurs within the home whether we like it or not, whether we try to avoid it or not, but is also a *conscious* and highly *deliberate* process for the caring family as it watches the children, in the safety and sanctity of their own home, test out, ask, feel, keep and tell secrets, and thereby grow and mature.

To be sure, the family of today, weakened by mobility, crises in communication, and a high divorce rate, and thus highly defensive about its role in a modern society, is hurting. It need not assume and should not let anyone foist upon it unnecessary burdens and roles. However, the role of value-setter is already "upon it," inherent in it, even if and when the family protests and attempts to "evict" the children—especially the small children—to institutions which consciously or unconsciously usurp its own educational role. Arnold Toynbee is quoted by educator George B. Leonard as saying about formal education in America: "It degenerated . . . into book learning divorced from a spontaneous apprenticeship for life. . . . In fact, the art of playing with words was substituted for the art of living."[1] Leonard points out that in primitive cultures education was sacramental. That is, every aspect and event in life was related, had sacred meaning and values. Everything was not only observed but also experienced in a kind of wholeness or unity.[2] The family was central in the sacramental process.

Now we live in fragments, bits and pieces, and because we seem so unsure of our own values and how they relate "sacramentally," we are also unsure that we are the ones to pass on our muddled ideas, half-truths, vague hopes, and often, shattered dreams to our children. How sad. But does this not suggest the need for *adult* education in our culture and especially in the Christian parish?

VALUES IMPLEMENTATION

If it has been true that throughout history the passing of values to children and youth has been a natural occurrence within the ordinary and basic structures of everyday family life, including religious values and attitudes, then is it not good and right to attempt to recover, to resensitize, to touch once again, the very heart of values implementation for Christian education?

What does it mean for a child to choose a value for his or her life? Can values become part of a young life by and through persuasion, rules, reward and punishment, authority as persuader, appeal to conscience, lecture or moralizing? We engage in most all of these processes, sometimes with

1. George B. Leonard, *Education and Ecstasy* (New York: Delta Books, 1968), p. 11.
2. Ibid., p. 11.

results which are mutually satisfying and sometimes with mutual frustrations.

We know that parents cannot give a child faith, or even teach a child faith, much less give or teach anything of basic attitudinal certainty. Children are not to be vaccinated or injected. They remain persons in development; fragile and in great need of testing, finding parameters, and resolving issues and feelings by experiencing a good many things in life that we as parents would probably like them to avoid experiencing.

So basic values implementation involves first and foremost the recognition that a young life is caught up in the protracted and risky process of choosing values, and is in continual need of parental support. Ego identity is being formed. A parent-child trust relationship is in tenuous development. On this point, Eric H. Erickson says:

> The parental faith which supports the trust emerging in the new born, has throughout history sought its institutional safeguard (and, on occasion, found its greatest enemy) in organized religion. Trust born of care is, in fact, the touchstone of the *actuality* of a given religion.[3]

It is clearly within the religious purview of parenting that the values which children are to choose are chosen *freely* and in the context of a "trust born of care." Only where choice is truly possible can a value result for the child.

Thoughtless choices are part of the risk inherent in the freedom we know must be part of the parent-child trust pattern. But there are clear parental values already established, acted out, given day-to-day understanding, and occasional articulation within the home. These are observed and thoughtfully considered as basic to the child's understanding of shared trust.

Children come also to "significate" certain values as being

---

3. Eric H. Erickson, *Childhood and Society* (New York: W. W. Norton & Company, 1950), p. 250.

their own, that is, to hold them dear, prize, esteem, and respect them. In time children even develop the ability to speak of these values, and to articulate the depth of their commitment to what has been arrived at in a context of parentally supported freedom and an atmosphere of trust.

PARENTS AND VALUES

If we as parents, nervous about the shattering, fast-paced world we live in, see ourselves as incapable of such a freedom/trust setting, then perhaps we had better look to a few roots or models for sustenance and help.

Visceral Beginnings

Most of us begin our "teacher" role as a parent. It is here, in parenting, that we learn the importance of exposing honest ignorance as well as profound learning. It is here that we recover sensitivity concerning our relationships to others, particularly as parents to children. It is here, in this setting, that we receive the unanswerable questions of youth which we do not wish trivialized by a well-meaning "other" adult.

Our son or daughter asks, "Who made God?" No need for frustrations now because we are not in an answer-oriented classroom but rather in a laboratory of living and feeling humans. The answer may be a simple "I don't know," followed by a comment concerning the importance of such a question, or by a brief conversation on the family's common search or even appreciation for the mystery behind the question. Parents give time and space to children so that the young may proceed with their own value implementation. To question together as a family is a *gift*, a rare gift difficult to duplicate in any other setting. It is to be cherished, not feared.

If we have abdicated the passing on of succinct stories—the very story of life and its various significations in our own lives—then it is about time we relearned the procedure. We

ּ5ּ7097

need to reassume the role which, despite our pretense of dependency upon a system, has been ours all along.

We have simply assumed too much from a delivery system. No alternate system can substitute for that which is essentially given over to the family. It cannot deliver the needed intimacy. It cannot relate the secrets of youth to the messages of human hope. It has no power to forgive—*really* forgive—nor to make incarnate the essential spirit of familial acceptance.

Robert O'Neil and Michael Donovan have spoken bluntly about the inability of the parenting-substitute to carry the necessary visceral freight in those early formative years of childhood:

> Formal religious education prior to adolescence implants idolatrous notions of God, gravely damages other basic religious concepts, and immunizes the child from genuine religious inquiry at the appropriate age.[4]

They admit to the possibility of rhetorical overkill, but point out that they reached such a conclusion only after intensive study of findings of the social and behavioral sciences along with an examination of contemporary educational practices.

A Biblical Model

There are indications within his own ministry that Jesus sensed the innate power, intimacy, and responsibility of the family. As we like to put it: "Jesus taught adults and played with children." This too says something about the fragile ability, even the inability, of children to deal with a formal or routine indoctrination of values.

Perhaps Jesus perceived such a "truth" all along in his ministry. I do not wish to make an exegetical case here, partly because I think it would be a difficult thing to do

4. Robert O'Neil and Michael Donovan, *Children, Church, and God* (New York: Corpus Publications, 1970), p. 9.

given the historical record in the Gospels, but mainly because my purpose is only to poke a few playful holes in our apparent dependency upon a system which we tend to make a "be all and end all" in our society.

Why can't we at least consider the possibility that creative and cerebral *education* happens to, with, from, and by *adults* and that formative basic values and Christian styles are set within the dynamic, however meager, of the home and family? Why must we insist on revamping, reorganizing, or rewriting the structural scripts or curriculum for the Sunday school and keep placing our hopes in a revival of a day gone by?

EDUCATION AND THE CHRISTIAN COMMUNITY

To say that the formal educational task is adult-oriented is also to say that it is the mutual task of the Christian community. We have found numerous opportunities and occasions at CCS to "educate" the young, especially when the community gathers for worship:

Advent themes of creating the new covenant are coupled with the telling of legends, myths, and stories from other countries to help the children to anticipate the Christ-mass event.

New Year's Eve sees us imitate the levitical custom of "release" of the burdens and unfulfilled dreams of the past year; we write them on paper, throw them into a big, black kettle, and just before the midnight eucharist we burn them, releasing the weight of the past and freeing ourselves for the future.

Epiphany is Twelfth Night, occasion for crowning the three "wise men" and letting the children order everyone around with commands of love as we share in the last of the Christmas carols, cookies, and wassail.

Lent offers opportunities to involve children in the common experience and feelings of those of the passion cast, the "stations" on Good Friday, the seder meal with Jewish friends on Palm Sunday or before the end of Holy Week, and the mystery and joy of the Easter Vigil.

All through the year the themes of Christian life invite us to play and be illumined by stories: A Celebration of the Feast of All Hallows (in which we spoof and make fun of death by masks and costumes), a liturgy on themes of hunger called "Their Names Are Today," from a poem by Gabriel Mistral, a liturgy of the innocents (dealing with those who innocently suffer, based on Herod's slaying of the children), a liturgy remembering the saints both common and friendly to our experiences, and a children's liturgy in celebration of animals. We have also provided helps for home worship, not typical "devotions" as such, but liturgical actions for celebrating birthdays, homecomings, overnight guests, baptismal birthdays, anniversaries, and a home eucharist.[5] It is a major responsibility of the church of course, local, regional, and national, to provide trained clergy for the community, "rabbis" whose main jobs are to be theologian-in-residence and enabler of genuine lay ministry in the world. A possible third clergy task might also be to enable lay people clearly to articulate the faith for themselves. The church must again recover the vital roles of teaching Scripture, interpreting the word in the world, and theological-prophetic commentary on the daily activities of humans in our neighborhoods and nations.

There are roles for the laity to play along with the trained clergy. These are roles which emanate from the style, profession, job, avocation, hobby, special interest, or occasional reading of interested adults who are willing to be vulnerable as co-theologians-in-residence. Lay persons can stand forth as human beings over against the still-popular image of the clergy as well-prepared answer machines; they can with eagerness and vigor raise up crucial issues and concerns for day-to-day living.

5. See Jack Lundin, *Little Liturgies for the Christian Family* (Downers Grove: CCS Publishing House, 1970), and Jack Lundin, *Celebrations for Special Days and Occasions* (New York: Harper & Row, 1971).

We have just about controlled, regulated, and routinized many people of creative mind and artistic talent right out of the church. Let us not make the same error with those thoughtful and sound adults who might otherwise wish to be utilized in more challenging capacities than chairing the "grounds" committee or passing the plate on Sunday.

At CCS we have depended upon both professional theologians and informed laity as our rabbis-in-residence. It has enlivened our corporate life and authenticated a part of the meaning of priesthood of believers. Lay persons have taught courses and led seminars on: "Lessons in History," "Death and Dying," "Unusual Books," "Abortion and Ethics," "Probing Parenting Problems," "Creative Writing," "Photography," "Film-making for Children and Teens," "Science and Faith," "Book Reviews," "Communication Tools and the Therapeutic Community," "International Life-views and Life-styles," "Rape," "Yoga," "Symbols, Words, and Colors," "Theology and Literature," "Theology and the Arts," "Music for the Fun of It," "Beethoven's Birthday Party," "Relating the History of Jazz to Developments in Civilization," "Humor in Theology and the Bible," and "Renaissance Christmas Art."

The Adult Guarantor

While I strongly defend family-oriented value implementation and the focus of formal Christian education on the adult years and the stages immediately preceding them, I would wish quickly to point out that such a proposed structuring ought not to be set in concrete. There are a number of "guarantors" which the structural church can provide the family through the children's formative years.

By providing adult guarantors we mean continually to discover the importance of the identity struggle with small and growing children, and to make available to those children adults whom the children can respect and value as dependable. A child gains in being with people who genuinely "like me." The adult guarantor should be someone who, as Albert van den Heuvel puts it,

> notices personally and uniquely a particular person, talks to him as an equal, and by his manner enables the young person to feel, "being the kind of person I am, I will make it." The guarantor is experienced primarily as "one who enjoys me, thinks I am worthy of being listened to and understood, a person I click with."[6]

The Wednesday Children's Program

As a support to parents, CCS tries to provide opportunity for authenticating adults or "adult guarantors" to be available to the children and to identify themselves as part of the larger listening, empathetic, and therapeutic Christian community. Every Wednesday from 4:15 to 5:15 p.m. there is a Children's Program which we have tried carefully to conceive and shape.

In it the pastor takes time for children in ways that are nearly impossible on Sunday mornings. The children have the right to know the pastor as a human being, story-teller, and dependable friend. The hour is divided between "pastor's time" (for story-telling, listening, and sharing) and time with other dependable adults in graded classrooms.

Insofar as possible, the classroom activities avoid competitiveness. No child is asked to "know something" in order to find acceptance. Each child is appreciated and accepted by virtue of his or her personhood.

Play, doing things with hands and body as well as minds and imagination, becomes part of the "curriculum." The adults in the program *become* the curriculum. Christianity is made as touchable and human as people may allow.

There is a conscious effort to avoid usurping the role of parent as primary teacher. The program, therefore, asks

6. Albert van den Heuvel, ed., *The New Creation and the New Generation* (New York: Friendship Press, 1965) , p. 39.

parents for involvement by providing things to do, talk about, act out, and read together in the home, things that relate to the Wednesday themes. The program also relies on parent feedback.

The "Plunge" Program

As youngsters begin genuinely to question, there should be specific educational structures available. At CCS, youngsters grow chronologically and in emotional and intellectual maturity they are given the opportunity to experience many exciting events *with* the church, not in isolation from it. We begin our more serious dialoguing with the sixth, seventh, and eighth graders on a wide range of subjects. "Valuing" occurs through active "plunges" into places, events, and life experiences. We may visit a synagogue and especially a bar mitzvah, or a pop symphony concert; an artist community or a Russian Orthodox Easter event and liturgy; a hospital communication center, the county jail, or a play or movie. We visit people of differing ethnic and religious values, eat our way through ethnic neighborhoods, spend a day on the farm, or visit with the special ministry pastor at the local race track.

The plunge is supportive of family value-setting but also supports the children as they now begin to experience the terror of occasionally opposing parental views and feelings: "Is it alright for me to be me, even when that is different from values I perceive as 'OK' at home?" No one can suffer through for another the pains of adolescence, least of all parents. Values are already fairly well set. Trust is either evidencing itself or not. It is time for *more* to happen. It is time for adult guarantors to be available, and for the church to be as caring and supportive through these fidgety and stressful years.

It has been my experience that youngsters will share occasional secrets. They may disclose uncertainty about themselves, or risky relationships with others, to test out once again my guarantor role with them and to let their inner selves know that it is safe for them to own such feelings. It is good and necessary for such emotions, even such unease, to be an acknowledged part of the Christian community's mutual task and life together.

First Confirmation

By the time ninth graders are ready for their "basic year"[7] of study leading toward their making their "first confirmation,"[8] there is a realization on the part of most youngsters that formal or cerebral Christian education is an ongoing process, a yet to be discovered and dynamic attitude which will continue to ferment all through one's life.

We have deliberately coined the term "first confirmation" in order that the implications might be understood and felt. How often do we hear pastors and laity complain that confirmation seems like the *end* of an educational process for many youngsters instead of an exciting beginning of a lifelong reevaluative process? It need not be so if the questionable assumptions spoken of at the beginning of this chapter are scrapped and we begin to deal with children's *visceral* needs in early life instead of stuffing them full of facts and biblical data (out of parental paranoia?) until they regurgitate what we want to hear from them on their confirmation day, only to hear from them no more, for they have "graduated" from the church.

By the time a young teenager, or even an older child, makes a truly *first* confirming of faith, there is also the acknowledgment that such a con-*firm*-ing is firm only in the same way that any honest person's faith is firm—as it is able

7. The "basic year" program includes fifteen three-hour sessions concerning biblical interpretation and content, meanings of basic doctrines and biblical themes, life as sacrament, worship as life-drama, the life and teachings of Christ, history and purposes of the church, and the meaning of risk in living the committed life in covenant with Christ.

8. Not to be confused with children's "first communion" which is usually received many years earlier and usually when a child is ready, parents are supportive, and the pastor is in agreement that the child's motives are honest. The Eucharist has no educational string attached. It is not earned by "knowing" anything!

to know, handle, and realize the depths of concomitant *un-faith*. The father in Mark's gospel proclaimed his belief while at the same time admitting to his unbelief. Jacob wrestled with the angel of his unfaith in order to discover anew the faith which he could not leave to his father and grandfather but had to make his. Again we reside in the dialectic which, all along, we hold up as the necessary tension-filled crucible in which life is lived. Growth is to be expected, therefore, not in isolation but in tension.

We learn love from the evidence of our need to recover from the unlove in us. We share love with another person through the inevitability of the pain which such genuine love will bring along with it. We do not live in Camelot but in a real world in which the dialectic is continually played out. There is no escape. There is only the painful-joyous reassessing and growing in a grace which, coming from God, refuses to protect us from sin and pain but rather insists that we discover precisely in such alienating powers our need for reconciliation and the joy of his Presence.

No one of us may be coerced into a posture of authentic faith. This is why the educational task of the church is not automatically akin to that of the educational task of the public school.

Youngsters who come to "know the right things" may have been catechized, but not much more. Christianity is obviously not a collection of correct doctrines or even good and meaningful stories.

We are God's people only because he has said so. But we can also come to know that simple truth only by struggle, and in a step-by-step lifelong process in which care is taken to avoid crushing, manipulating, or overwhelming the spirit of response, the realities of the love-hate we feel toward God at various times in our lives, and the tender care we must offer each other as Christ's people open to the future.

7. The Public Church: Power and Servanthood

A community that lacks reconciliation destroys itself through fratricide. A community that lacks prophetic criticism destroys itself through immobility.

—Michael Novak,
A Theology for Radical Politics

If with Christ you died to the elemental spirits of the universe, why do you live as if you still belonged to the world? —Colossians 2:20

For everyone who does not know how to control his inmost self would feign control his neighbor's will according to his own conceit. —Goethe, *Faust*

Yes, God loved the world so much that he gave his only Son. —John 3:16 (JB)

THE PUBLIC VS. THE PRIVATE CHURCH

It is hoped that in the church we have had done with hanging superficial labels on institutions and people; labels such as "liberal" and "conservative," especially as they have been used to describe denominational bodies and particular congregations. Most people are mixtures of both. We might be politically liberal while holding to strict views on conservation of natural resources. We might be for fiscal responsibility and a balanced budget while advocating unlimited spending on certain projects we regard as crucial.

Many people have begun to see denominations and congregations as the complicated amalgams they truly are.

There has also been an effort to find satisfactory ways of describing them. One such descriptive model, which projects some clarity as to what the church is about and how it expresses its biblical mandate and self-understanding, is that of the public church/private church.

The private church is concerned with vertical relationship; that is, relationship with God. It sometimes rejects as "worldly" political and social concerns. Often the private church tends to see the world either as that which must be transformed or as that which must be denied. There are other viewpoints somewhere between these two extremes but in general suffice it to say, the private church sees itself as standing over against the world; it projects clear images of this world as a "party of the opposition." The private church or the vertical church espouses what H. Richard Niebuhr calls the "Christ against culture" stance toward the world.[1]

Many western Christians have found the private, the vertical, attractive. It accords the Christian message and mandate a uniqueness or peculiarity that helps to separate Christians from the "worldly," sheep from goats, good from evil, and those who are singular in their "life in Christ" from those who succumb to the temptations of the sinful life. It is not a very large step from such distinctions to a picture of God as wishing to have relationship only with those select humans who, by grace or faith or works or whatever, place themselves in that private vertical relationship *as a way of doing his will* on earth.

The private church, therefore, considers Christian education a "plus" education. It equips people for the inevitable battle with the world which must be won.

The private church understands the word, the gospel, as directed to the relationship between Christ and the individual believer. It is often unwilling to trust other churches which "have to do" with the world.

1. H. Richard Niebuhr, *Christ and Culture* (New York: Harper and Brothers, 1951).

The private church "saves" people from the world for Christ. It speaks of pagan vices against Christian virtues. It all but ignores or explains away the first chapter of Genesis and the writer's insistence on seeing all of creation as good, even "very good." (Gen. 1:31).

The public church on the other hand, while interested in a mandate to save, assumes that salvation is not "from the world" but for service and servanthood styles within the world.

The public church hears the voice of the gospel both in the Gospel record and in the world in which God still chooses to work. In fact, the public church is often embarrassingly aware of God's repeated circumventing of "his people" as he chooses to work through the "outsider."

The public church views Christian education as an unending process of questioning and learning. It is particularly wary of dogmatic or absolutizing approaches to the understanding of life.

The public church understands its call toward relationship with God *not only* in the vertical sense but *as often* in the horizontal relationships: "As you did it to one of the least of these my brethren . . ." (Matt. 25:40).

Guilt and Love

The examples of guilt and love, both of which involve relationship, may help us to understand the differences/connections between the private church and the public church. There are necessary tensions between the two, but it is also important to exercise care in appropriating, or better in keeping in tension, both styles.

It sometimes becomes tempting to let ourselves get so caught up in guilt toward God, or even toward the institution of the church, that we spare ourselves the anguish of having to deal concretely with the very real guilt we ought to feel toward our fellow humans. If "guilt before God" is the only possible guilt, then there is hardly anything to stop us from justifying certain actions toward each other which impartial onlookers might consider unjust, merciless, and even cruel. Unfortunately too many liturgical expressions in our western churches have given support to the notion that our guilt before God stands as a separate reality. This, of course, does not square with the gospel, which clearly involves a both/and set of relationships: both God and neighbor.

It is also tempting to speak much about our love for God. The Bible speaks rather of the love of God, saying that he is love and that he loves us. Rarely is there an isolated injunction for humans to love God. Biblically such a command is commonly accompanied by injunctions on how such love may be actualized in mercy or justice or an act of response to some particular human need or situation. God does not need our isolated adoration.

In fact, quite apart from Scripture, is it psychologically or sociologically even possible for a human to love God? Is it not more to the point—even of the biblical message—that we humans learn to *trust* God and *love* each other?

Tension and Paradox

Martin Luther places what we have thus far called the tensions of relationship or the dialectic in a paradox: the life in Christ or the "kingdom of God's right hand" is expressive of the vertical relationship, while the life in culture or the "kingdom of God's left hand" denotes the horizontal relationship. Though closely related, the two are clearly distinguished. The Christian, therefore, affirms both "in a single act of obedience to the one God of mercy and wrath, not as a divided soul with a double allegiance and duty."[2]

The tension or paradox described here is powerfully expressed by Michael Novak when he deals with the dangerous business of being a Christian amid the power structures and principalities of this world:

> To be a Christian is to stand within this people and to benefit by its traditions, its liturgy, its symbols, its wisdom,

2. Niebuhr, *Christ and Culture*, p. 172.

and its fellowship. But to stand within this people as if the goals of the Community were to glorify itself, or to establish limits for human development, would be to betray the Word. Creation must not be subordinated to redemption. The world must not be subordinated to the church. The Word is already present in creation, already present in the world. Christians do not "bring" Jesus to the world; he is already there. They go to speak to the world, the relationship is dialogical, and they announce the Word truthfully only if they listen for the presence of the Word already there: abyss cries out to abyss. The missionary enterprise ought not to be a venture in modestly disguised arrogance; it ought to be a venture of discovery.[3]

Models for Servanthood

The very nature of the tension described by Luther, Novak, and others causes us to question older models of parish life which may be geared to serving either the private church or the public church exclusively.

Because we need to know and hear Christ already in our world and because we meet him so often in the needs and hopes and pains and joys of each other, we know also that such needs and hopes very often form or culminate in institutions and structures that are self-serving as well as self-giving. How shall we address ourselves then to such organizations and structures such as government, business, industry, church? Are these structures to be of little or no importance to the Christian?

For many congregations that question has clearly been answered in the affirmative. We have given ourselves over to the building of parochial structures or private organizations within the local church itself to the exclusion of interrelationships with the very real power structures of our society. Parish constitutions seem to demand such intramural organizations. But the social ministry committee, for one, is essentially powerless since it has no meaning to anyone except its own members of the parish board to whom it is responsible. It

3. Michael Novak, *A Theology for Radical Politics* (New York: Herder and Herder, 1969), p. 120.

may, upon occasion, study a social issue and recommend that the congregation take action through signing petitions, writing congressmen, or otherwise acting out roles of ombudsman or lobbyist, but rarely does it function to involve members of the congregation in the actual struggle as a group investing real power in a real world in which real decisions are made that really affect masses of humans.

Since the model for servanthood in the world—as over against a servanthood merely within the congregation—requires structuring beyond the dictates of the parish constitution on standing committees, we at CCS decided to become "issue oriented" in our basic parish structuring and life. We felt compelled to a complete rethinking of how we might maintain good order within the community, skipping the frills yet serving ourselves in the mutual task of being "built up together in Christ," while we at the same time streamline the machinery for servanthood, finding ways to remind each other of the dangers and enticements of merely "playing church" with ourselves. Structures emerged as a result of that rethinking:

1. Each Sunday we take time for what we call "pre-liturgy," a period in which issues, concerns, and feelings are aired and communications are heard from members of the covenant and from visitors as well.

2. If two or more members wish to engage in a "ministry" as a result of our having given attention to an issue or concern, we acknowledge it to be a part of CCS' common life.

3. When people say, "Don't mix politics and church" they mean partisan politics but certainly not the substantive issues at the heart of our political systems. There is no way around taking firm sides in human issues, political, social, or any other.

4. The whole congregation, in pre-liturgy each Sunday of the year, holds the decisional power, whether by vote or by silent acceptance. It is the determining body in all matters of ministry and servanthood toward ourselves and others. This has allowed us to enter into ventures and

risks which no small representative governing body could ever do.

5. Since the congregation each week is the decision-making group, the church council and its tasks are necessarily redefined. The council becomes voluntary and is formed anew at the beginning of each new covenant year. It has the tasks of maintaining the ongoing life/order of CCS, collecting data pertinent to issues of concern, and causing both interaction and communication to take place between CCS ministries and all covenant members.

The pre-liturgy functions quite well from Sunday to Sunday, year in and year out. It has kept decisional power (those who "run" the church) in the hands of the whole community. Nothing is discussed or decided in secret, not even within the confines of an elected representative group. Everyone feels a part of the Community because everyone clearly has opportunity not only to "know what's going on" but also to help make it happen.

THE CHURCH AND POWER

The Meaning of Power

Rollo May quotes Emily Dickinson as saying "to be alive is power,"[4] meaning, of course, that we as humans are unique pulsating power plants in and of ourselves. But May defines the power used by the human as the ability to cause or prevent change.[5]

In psychological terms, power may be easily identified with one's being. Tillich's "power of being," Nietzsche's "will to power," Bergson's *élan vital* all, in one way or another, express such a life process. Power is also a sociological term and serves as a category to describe wars, conflicts, and national movements. Power has been a usable term for nearly

4. Rollo May, *Power and Innocence* (New York: W. W. Norton, 1972), p. 99.
5. Ibid., p. 99.

every human discipline because everywhere change of some kind is taking place.

For the church too, and its theology, power is the ability to act, to grow, to change, but there is additionally a spiritual dimension whereby, in the final picture, all power is attributed to God. It is God whose creative energy makes the earth and all that is! And it is God whose power is also loosed or given to those who wish to promote his Kingdom on earth! A number of biblical images point to power being appropriated both personally and corporately in Yahweh's name or in Christ's name. The implication is that power is not only used by God in a continuing kind of creative energy for life itself, but that power may, under circumstances beyond our understanding and control, be used by his servants in the actualization of his will.

The history of the Christian church is replete with times and occasions when the church has felt the call from God himself to appropriate temporal power in Christ's name and for the "good" of the people. Historically, there are also times when the church pulls back from any use of temporal power, times even when it may be unsure of the meaning of spiritual power. We can easily be embarrassed by our use of power but also by our apparent impotency to act for change except within the canons and rubrics of personal piety. It is no surprise that the church has always struggled for clearer definitions and mandates toward use of earthly power.

Power *will* be used, even if individually or corporately we think to avoid it. But what kind of power—that is the question. May's categories include the usual: exploitative, manipulative, and competitive (all of which are interwoven into the commonly understood expectations and dreams of civil religion). He also speaks of nutrient power (that which is fostered in home and church, is exercised for the sake of the *other,* and is thus acceptable and praiseworthy in the eyes of the beholder). It is May's last category, integrative power, that we must learn to use once again in our generation and world.[6]

Integrative power *abets* my neighbor's power. This it does, paradoxically, by opposing in the manner of a devil's advocate another's use of power. It causes the other person to think—and feel—about his use of power in order to avoid the thoughtlessness of the exploitative and the manipulative and the accidental paternalism of the nutrient. It is, in essence, a power of and through the questioning process, a process which, as we have seen, the church needs and is trying to revive. The value to the speaker of audience questions, even critical queries, is immense. It triggers fresh insight, renews purpose, exposes dimensions not yet considered, and, importantly from the Christian point of view, affects how *people* are valued *vis à vis* any particular usage of human power. May says:

> I was tempted to call this kind of power "cooperative" but I realized it too often begins with the "victim" having to be coerced into the cooperation. Our narcissism is forever crying out against the wounds of those who would criticize us or point out our weak spots. We forget that the critic can be doing us a considerable favor. Certainly criticisms are often painful and one has to brace oneself in the face of them. We can slide back into manipulative power (by forcefully silencing the critic) or competitive power (by making the critic look silly). Or we can even protect our thin skins by means of nutrient power (patronizing the critic by implying he is confused and needs our care). But if we do regress in these ways, we are losing an opportunity for new truth that the questions, hostile or friendly as the case may be, may well be giving us.[7]

Though May speaks of integrative power more on the psychological than the sociological level, his model can

6. Ibid., pp. 105–13.
7. Ibid., pp. 109–10.

apply to the church's understanding of missional tasks in its ministry to, with, and from the world. We can easily recall how defensive the church can be, has been, and undoubtedly will be in its silencing of the critic. It has attempted to make the critic look silly. It has declared the critic to be outside of the "truth," beyond the pale of orthodoxy. It has been especially fond of patronizing the "outsider's" fuzzy thinking. Integrative power leads to growth, however, because it does not presume outsider/insider mentalities but, using the dialectic or dynamic process which continually pushes for clarity of understanding, sets forth a questioning procedure very much like that of Jesus in his ministry.

A Biblical Model

The questioning or "integrative" use of power was part of Jesus' radical ministry. It had him proclaiming a "too moral" interpretation of the law at one time and a "not moral enough" interpretation another time.

In the Sermon on the Mount (especially Matt. 5:20–48), Jesus works toward a proclamation of salvation which presupposes a radical interpretation of the law, an acknowledgment that the Kingdom was taking place within his own ministry and that he was making Kingdom relationships work with, of all people, social outcasts and those impossible to categorize as law-keepers. Jesus abrogates the law, goes beyond it, makes it ridiculous to use as a sole weapon for social justice or even for a justification of rightness of position on issues of morality and living.

While he fulfilled the law in the depth of its religious meaning in his own being and his death on the cross, he, in his life, broke the ceremonial laws and challenged other religious observances that people easily use to turn their attention away from the real issues and the need for justice and reconciliation. Religious people rarely like being jolted out of their well-established and often formalized routines, even to be interrupted by the world's needs. Jesus knew this. His own ministry was untypical in the sense that the world's needs were heard ahead of rituals, laws, and regulations. His call to reform was not couched in terms of patching up any existing religious mentality; it struck rather at the very heart of the status quo and the unthinking use of power.

The possibility for the church to "afflict the comfortable" as well as "comfort the afflicted" (we do the latter more comfortably than the former) is inherent in the biblical model. Like Jesus, the church can be more concerned with a person's integrity and with compassion being exercised than with a person's orthodoxy and with piety being observed.

Our goal at CCS is to help people come to touch the real issues, the places of their personal and social integrity, especially as that integrity has to do with the gospel. We use liturgical themes throughout the year to educate, and to provide us with themes for dialogue. Within the traditional framework of the eucharistic liturgy we have focussed on seeing Christ in places, people, and events (the Christmas Eve themes of Incarnation); on human authenticity (through an examination of the motives of the passion cast); on liberation (listening to Third World voices); on national lamentation and themes of work and leisure.

LAITY AS CHRIST INCOGNITO

We speak often at CCS about "being a Christ incognito in the marketplace." This is a way of implementing the biblical model, practising the questioning, confrontational, integrative use of power, whether individually or corporately, in a way that can be identified as Christian in its nature and thrust.

Without fanfare we enter already existing structures where real issues are being decided and where power translates into expenditures of money or influence. *Instead of* belonging to a congregational committee which has power only to *talk* about the various structures of power, usually with appropriate lamentations and/or anger, we actually participate in political parties, local community government, school boards, and community organizations such as the ACLU, mental health boards, and open housing coalitions.

Lay Ministry

The laity too have a ministry. Most clergy have been trained, or at least expected, to play out the role of entrepreneur, quite independent of the laity. The pastor often speaks of his or her ministry as that which lay persons may see as including, absorbing, or usurping their own. This is tragic both for the ordained minister and for the laity. If the clergy must "do" the ministry for the congregation then reconciliation, forgiveness, renewal, social justice, and even the giving and receiving of love are reduced to parodies and sham. Both clergy and laity are thereby demeaned.

The clergy must once again have restored the twin roles of rabbi (teacher and interpreter of the word) and enabler (commentator on the real ministry in the world being carried out by every lay person). Both clergy and laity need their dignity restored. Both need their ministry: the clergy as one who helps point to, define, and give support to the ministries of the faithful; and the lay person as the one who knows, "owns," and can articulate his or her ministry in a real world.

To accomplish such restoration of roles within the church the clergy must give up their usurpation and "handling" of the great variety of ministries to the world. This is not to suggest an abdication of the clergy roles of eucharistic celebrant or chief interpreter of the word along with other expected in-parish duties such as marrying and burying. Although even many of these functions in worship and interpretation need to be shared with the laity, it is the assumed roles of pastoral leadership in areas beyond in-parish functioning that must come under renewed scrutiny. Let the clergy *accompany* the laity into the world, into investigation of issues, into the political arena, into the questioning process, and into the most critical and socially sharpened use of integrative power, that of the community organization with its techniques for confronting the powers and principalities regarding those everyday issues which concern us all.

Community Organization

Let it be clearly understood by one and all that those who "bring Christ into the world" are not only the clergy but, most impressively, the laity. And when the issues have been identified and understood, and the controlling human powers also identified, understood, *and confronted,* then let the clergy help the laity raise the important question of "In whose name did we now act?" The answer may evoke reevaluation or repentance. It also may lead to celebration of the real Presence of Christ in the real conflicts and issues of people.

A few years ago a layman from CCS, David Veatch, received denominational sponsorship for a yearlong training in community organization through the Industrial Areas Foundation in Chicago. The late Saul Alinsky, president and founder of IAF, had been asked by various denominations to help selected clergy understand the principles of "issue orientation" and how people of diverse ideology, people who know that they have no appreciable "power base" other than the power of the lone vote, can be convened simply on the basis of where they hurt and wish to see creative change take place in our society.

A successful accountant, David Veatch was to become the only layman in that group. He helped us to see that vested interest is not necessarily bad, and that self-interest is not all that holds a community organization together. It is true that sometimes the private citizen's rights may be co-opted or assumed by political power structures, especially those which operate in a "machinelike" way. Beyond the vote, the only way to make corrective changes, defend rights, and help elected officials or others in power positions know what public and/or enlightened will is, is to use integrative power in the face of the power of the status quo.

Clergy and laity alike have, we trust, more than just vested interest in such participation—they constitute the church! There are enlightened and informed values and issues for which prophets would risk personal reputation and for which Jesus himself risked death and humiliation. Publicly to articulate and work for them is part of the "commentary," the living interpretation of those who would bear witness to faith in Jesus Christ.

Community organization of course is not a "be all, solve all" in any purview of the church's program of social ministry. It is, however, for too many contemporary Christians either a scary and repugnant "tool of the radicals" or simply an untried and unexamined option which many parishes feel they are not structurally equipped to deal with, much less bring into focus.

At CCS, community organization developed under the leadership of Dave Veatch. It has had many ups and downs, frustrating beginnings, and sagging middles. We discovered that a true community organization does not consist of a single issue accompanied by those folks interested only in that one issue. Community organizations are made up of great numbers of issues and concerns which great numbers of diverse and pan-political people bring to the group as a whole. There may be only a few dozen people interested in quality education and probable tax increases, as compared with the many who complain about taxes being too high and who are content with the educational level as it is. How are these few going to voice their concern and assure that the issue gets at least a fair hearing by power structures in control of local educational standards and by the general public? The community organization helps at this point, not because education is everybody's issue, but because a few people are willing and able to bring integrative power to bear.

Our local community organization, of which CCS is a dues-paying corporate member, is called the United Citizens Organization. Its concerns include fair taxation, flood control in the county, exploitation by land developers, unethical practices on the part of county officials (UCO was chiefly instrumental in causing a high county public official to be indicted for fraud), and a myriad of local issues which people feel they can touch and help guide and determine. "Local" is a word dear to the hearts of community organization people, second only to "issue." It is obviously important for others as well, and might become so for church people. For many years, the managing editor of the *Chicago Daily News* had a sign on his desk that read, "If It Isn't Local, It Isn't Real." He knew where and about what people really care. So must the church.

Epilogue

The reader will have noted throughout that I have used a number of key terms to describe the theological understanding and common life of CCS. These terms bespeak crucial elements of the Christian dynamic.

By "tension" I have meant to hold up in the most constructive of ways the necessity of dealing with opposing ideas. By "dialectic" I mean to use in a nonpolitical sense a commonly misunderstood term and point to a continual awareness of the antithetical and the need for every new synthesis. By "paradoxical" I simply point to a heritage from Luther with which we need again to become conversant: learning from those truths which are set in opposition to each other but which must never be allowed to immobilize us or, for the sake of convenience, nudge our witness into some comfortable middle position. By "dialogue" I raise up those conversations which keep us open to the future. Depending upon the context and nature of the conversation, I suppose I would want to use all of those words—tension, dialectic, paradox, dialogue—to describe the dynamic of the church open to the ever-changing and ever-surprising future.

Jesus was a harbinger of creative change, and his ministry brought a new dimension, a new hope, to those who thought about themselves and their lives in relationship to God. He gave them reason to go beyond law, beyond cult, beyond their own understanding, beyond their own commitments, beyond themselves and their structures. He called them into a new dynamic in which faith learns from unfaith; in which there is a difficult kind of tension between insiders and outsiders; in which a new sense of vulnerability and ordinariness and spontaneity all offer up fresh and unexpected gifts to a faith that is embedded in life; in which restlessness and curiosity replace dependency and absolutes; in which worship exposes us to ourselves as *homo ludens* (playful people) and God as the one who invites us to live out our resurrection *now*; in which there is no guarantee that our faith will survive unless we offer it up into a genuine struggle to keep rediscovering; in which we share trust with the young and the wisdom of such trusting with adults; in which there is no available measuring tool for worth other than the whimsical perspectives of a grace and devotion which God has for us and which, while causing us to pause in restored wholeness, insistently pushes us into being a church for an open future.